Battleship *Texas*

NUMBER FORTY-FIVE

Centennial Series of the Association of Former Students,
Texas A&M University

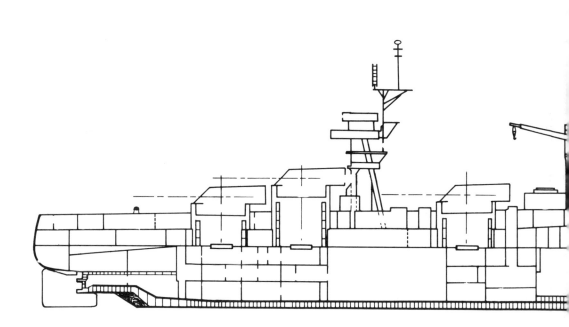

BATTLESHIP
TEXAS

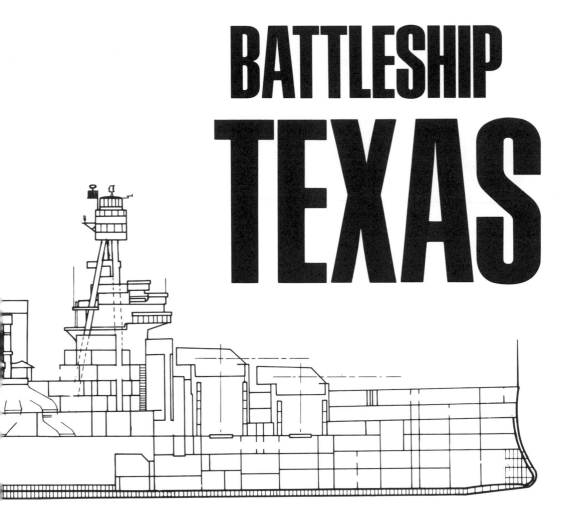

TEXT AND CONTEMPORARY PHOTOGRAPHS BY **Hugh Power**

INTRODUCTION BY JOHN REILLY

FOREWORD BY WILSON E. DOLMAN III, ORION KNOX, AND SUE WINTON MOSS

Texas A&M University Press
COLLEGE STATION

The paper used in this book meets the minimum requirements
of the American National Standard for Permanence
of Paper for Printed Library Materials, Z39.48-1984.
Binding materials have been chosen for durability. ∞

Library of Congress Cataloging-in-Publication Data

Power, Hugh Irvin, 1947–
    Battleship Texas / text and contemporary photographs by Hugh Irvin
Power, Jr. ; introduction by John Reilly ; foreword by Wilson E.
Dolman III, Orion Knox, and Sue Winton Moss.
        p.   cm. — (Centennial series of the Association of Former
Students, Texas A&M University ; no. 45)
    Includes index.
    ISBN 0-89096-516-1 (cloth). — ISBN 0-89096-519-6 (paper)
    1. Texas (Battleship)   I. Title.   II. Series.
VA65.T44P68   1992
359.3'2—dc20   92-7432
                                                                   CIP

To my wife, Betty,
  who nurtured it;
to A. C. Becker, Jr.,
  who guided it;
to Margarita Marders and Edwin Phillips,
  who inspired it;
and to Drs. Bernard Milstein and Harry Kelso,
  who made it possible,
  this book is gratefully dedicated.

Contents

Illustrations

Foreword

Participant in all the important naval theaters of the first half of the twentieth century, the battleship *Texas* is now a rare relic of the dreadnought era, when big ships with big guns were the most powerful weapons on earth. At the end of World War II, Texans, led by a schoolchildren's campaign, rallied to bring their namesake home, and *Texas* became the nation's first memorial battleship in 1948. Because of the ship's long operational history and unique status as a first-generation dreadnought, the "Mighty T" has been designated a National Historic Landmark. In addition, its two reciprocating steam engines are National Historic Engineering Landmarks. It is now moored alongside the Houston Ship Channel opposite the San Jacinto Monument, which marks the site of the Texas army's victory over Mexican forces in 1836.

Texas was reopened at its home berth on September 8, 1990, after a lengthy restoration in drydock. Restored to its appearance in 1945 when it supported the American landings at Iwo Jima and Okinawa, the ship serves as a tangible reminder of the price of freedom in the twentieth century.

In 1983 the Texas Legislature charged the Texas Parks and Wildlife Department with the responsibility of restoring and operating the battleship *Texas*. After a detailed study and evaluation of the ship's condition, a long-term plan was developed to guide repair and restoration. First on the list was the reestablishment of the watertight integrity of the ship's hull, decks, and superstructure. After sitting in the mud at San Jacinto for forty years, *Texas* was riddled with hull and piping leaks. A number of tanks were open to the sea, and water migrated fore to aft and back again through the deteriorating fuel and water piping systems. The wood decking had been replaced in the late 1960s with concrete, but instead of shedding water, the concrete acted like a sponge, and the steel splinter deck supporting the concrete was shot through with holes that let rainwater pass through to the decks below.

On December 13, 1988, *Texas* left its slip at San Jacinto under tow for drydock at Todd Shipyard in Galveston. During the ten-hour journey, the ship took on water in its midsection under the engine rooms. By the time Galveston was in sight, its draft nearly exceeded that of the drydock; only six inches' clearance remained as it was maneuvered onto the docking blocks. The yard's floating drydock came up slowly during the next eighteen hours, and water at first spewed, then dribbled, from blister and bottom tanks all along the hull. By the time work on the ship's hull was completed, nearly 350,000 pounds of corroded steel had been replaced with new plates, representing just under 15 percent of the hull's surface. More than forty thousand rivets were seal-welded to further ensure the hull's watertightness.

As work on the hull progressed, the shipyard also carried out other crucial repairs. The concrete decks were particularly stubborn. A giant jackhammer mounted on a small tractor broke the concrete into chunks, and workers using hand tools followed behind to clean up. During the ship's service career and at San Jacinto, the decks had a fore-to-aft trim, or slope, so afterdeck areas were the most severely corroded. Large sections of the rusted deck were cut out and replaced. Those sections with historical "footprints" of machinery and equipment were saved to become part of the ship's artifact collection. Sections of the piping and sounding tube systems were modified or repaired to aid maintenance monitoring. Major restoration work was done on the mainmast and foremast; decks and bulkheads were repaired; bulwarks were straightened; and doors and hatches were reworked and refitted.

When the structural work was complete, a modern epoxy coating was applied to the underwater hull to retard corrosion. An epoxy-alkyd system was sprayed above waterline, restoring the deep blue Camouflage Measure 21 paint scheme *Texas* wore in the Pacific in 1945.

Watertight once again, *Texas* headed out of Galveston on February 23, 1990, for an interim berth at Houston's Green's Bayou. Along the way it passed San Jacinto, where a permanent berth was being redeveloped. As part of the ship's rehabilitation, a new mooring system was built to allow the ship to float in the slip. Before, it had been hard aground, tied with wire lines to moorings on shore. The new system, safer and more secure, permits divers to monitor the condition of the ship's bottom and to do routine repairs. The slip itself was widened and deepened, and four mooring piles were driven seventy feet into the mud. *Texas* is now secured to the piles by four steel collars, anchored to withstand hurricane winds of 120 miles per hour.

While *Texas* was at Green's Bayou, installation of a new wood deck began. Pine planks, three and one-half inches square and up to twelve feet long, were fitted along the main deck in the historical pattern. To complete the new camouflage color scheme, the deck was painted the grayish blue called for by Camouflage Measure 21.

Restored to its former grandeur, *Texas* returned to San Jacinto on July 26, 1990. More than five thousand people lined the shore as tugs maneuvered it into the enlarged slip. Final preparations for reopening began as it lay in the shadow of the San Jacinto Monument once again. Cleaning and painting on the second deck and in the starboard engine room were completed, and the ship's brass and interpretive signs were reinstalled. Its silver services also were cleaned and polished. Those magnificent silver pieces are once again on display in the wardroom, along with the ship's trophies and other memorabilia.

Texas reopened on September 8, 1990. Gov. William P. Clements and First Lady Rita Clements led the salute to *Texas* that included the hoisting of the ship's colors and a memorable rendition of taps. Two days of festivities that weekend entertained more than twenty thousand visitors to the ship.

With the battle to save its structure won, *Texas* has entered a new era of public service, sound and watertight. The next phase of development is the restoration and interpretation of interior compartments. The project of room-by-room documentation, research, and restoration is aimed at the eventual interpretation of a small, floating city: the living and working spaces that supported a crew of more than eighteen hundred men fighting for the cause of freedom on both sides of the globe in World War II.

The success of the exterior restoration project, which has spanned almost seven years, is the result of the enthusiasm, support, and plain hard work of a number of people. The Battleship *Texas* Advisory Board, appointed by the governor of Texas to raise funds for the ship, marshaled contributions from the U.S. Navy, foundations, corporations, and private individuals throughout the state. The schoolchildren of Texas, whose predecessors in 1948 had so enthusiastically supported bringing the ship to San Jacinto, were among the prominent contributors for the most recent work. The Texas Parks and Wildlife Commission authorized the remainder of the restoration funds from park development moneys.

For five years before the shipyard work, *Texas'* own restoration and operational crews fought leaks and rust alongside volunteers from all walks of life. These crews and volunteers, bound by their common goal of preserving the "Mighty T," are still working, now devoting their attention to the meticulous restoration of interior compartments and working spaces.

Retired veterans of *Texas* inspired and encouraged the restoration workers by sharing their knowledge of the ship and their unique perspective on the history they made aboard it.

The true rewards that we all share and that bind us in our devotion to *Texas* are the personal satisfaction in having been part of this historic undertaking and the thrill of seeing the ship reflected once again in the eyes (and hearts) of the thousands of schoolchildren that walk its decks.

Texas Parks and Wildlife Department

WILSON E. DOLMAN III
ORION KNOX
SUE WINTON MOSS

Preface

The holodeck of the starship *Enterprise* has little in common with any part of the battleship *Texas*, but a moment involving the dreadnought of the future made up my mind to do this book about the dreadnought of the past.

For those who are not "Trekkies"—persons zealously devoted to, and turgidly knowledgeable about, the television series "Star Trek" (1966–68) and "Star Trek: The Next Generation" (1987–present)—a word of explanation. The holodeck, a new feature on the *Enterprise* of the current TV series, is a playground for adults. There, through holographic imaging, crew members can generate their fondest fantasies by simply programming the ship's computer. But this is too good a toy to remain a mere trivia footnote, and the series' writers have found a host of ways to involve the holodeck in episode plots. During one such episode, in that time wasteland left to advertising, my wife Betty asked me what my holodeck fantasy would be. She says it took me less than a minute to pick the place and time: the bridge of Adm. David Beatty's flagship, the battlecruiser HMS *Lion*, at 1600 hours (4 P.M.) on May 31, 1916.

Holodeck fantasies are usually selected for their pleasant and relaxing aspects, but the place and time I had chosen were anything but pleasant and restful. At that moment in history, *Lion* was leading six British Grand Fleet battlecruisers at twenty-seven knots through a sea erupting with unnerving regularity in fountains of water that towered above the ship's masts, the splashes of large-caliber German shells that had mercifully missed their target. These were the first moments of what historians call the run to the south, the opening gambit of the Battle of Jutland (pronounced "Yoot-land"). It was the last great clash of massed battle fleets and the only time the dreadnought battleships, for which the world's navies paid so much, would ever fight as their creators intended. In the next twelve hours, nearly ten thousand men would die, the German High Seas Fleet would lose eleven ships, the Grand Fleet fourteen, including three battlecruisers, and nothing would be decided. The course of World War I, which these dreadnoughts, these ultimate weapons, had been built to decide, would not change.

My wife knows all this. She has sat, with the patience of

the martyrs, through my retelling and analyzing of Jutland more times than I care to admit. So her interpretation of my holodeck selection was an informed one, and she delivered it in the final seconds before we returned to that week's plight of the *Enterprise.*

"I think you'll have to do a book on the *Texas,*" she said. "You'll be intolerable until you do."

Books get born in such moments of brief, incisive perception, though I now believe they gestate somewhere within us until we cannot be rid of them unless we write them. Looking back, that's the way it was with this one. As a book idea, *Texas* has been with me since 1986, when I did three articles on its impending restoration for *InBetween,* a small alternative magazine then being published in Galveston. *Texas* itself has been with me much longer, I think. The ship has gone under other names: *Missouri, Bismarck, Yamato, King George V.* But the thing it embodies, the dreadnought battleship in all its tragic majesty and unfulfilled mythology, has been hanging around since I was eight years old. That was the Christmas my grandfather bought me my first plastic model. It was the battleship *Missouri,* on which the Japanese signed the surrender documents to end World War II and from the decks of which the United States launched cruise missiles at Iraq in 1991. There is something near-mythological about that, like Thor and his hammer riding a tank into battle. *Missouri,* with a planned life span of two decades, has been around since before I was born, and is still a viable instrument of war.

Think about it. The dreadnought lineage began in 1906, when the airplane was three years old. We have walked on the moon and sent probes to the stars since then, and the dreadnought is with us still. Few weapons save the longbow and sword have had that long a run, and none before have seen such changes in the lives of those who made them.

Anyway, that is where this book really started, with my model of *Missouri,* given by the man who most shaped my childhood. I did not actually see *Texas* for another two years, and I was somewhat disappointed when I did. The lines were not as sleek, the superstructure was not as imposing as *Missouri*'s. And what in the name of everything was that gun turret doing amidships?

But the ship grows on you. At age fourteen I saw it again, and I know now that I had mellowed. I remember my father asking if I liked it better this time, and I think I said it looked like its guns might be able to hit something. I did not know then, because my father did not much discuss the "war" part of his World War II, that he had seen it hurling shells at German positions in the days following D-Day and knew far better than I what those guns could hit.

Curiously, after I came to Galveston in 1968, I did not go to San Jacinto and the ship for nine years. Then one day in 1977 Betty and I went, not to see the ship, but to eat at the San Jacinto Inn next door. Back then, the inn was one of the state's premier seafood eateries, an all-you-can-eat experience that strained reason and belt buckles alike. That was our destination that day, but we were too early, and so we went aboard *Texas*. That was the first time I climbed into No. 3 14-inch turret. All my life I have been drawn to, yet terrified of, great machinery. And I did not stay long in the dark, paint-peeled recess of the left gun sleeve. But for the first time, I felt something about the ship that stepped beyond dates and facts.

We went more often after that. Jokingly, I called *Texas* "The Shrine." My interest in history, dormant since my high school years, reemerged, and I began to read the story of these great, flawed ships called dreadnoughts.

It may be that their story is, as Shakespeare wrote, "a tale told by an idiot, full of sound and fury, signifying nothing." In its original intent, the dreadnought battleship was a failure, too powerful to be used well, too vulnerable to be decisive. Yet the story intrigues, catches us up in it, like the over-curious insect that wanders too near the spider's web. I have never known anyone to recover from dreadnought fever. When I was ten, I pitted my fleets of plastic dreadnoughts against my next-door neighbor's fleets of plastic aircraft carriers. He always won. He had history on his side. Yet I never felt defeated and never traded in a *Hood* or *New Jersey* for a *Wasp* or *Lexington*. There is loyalty among dreadnought zealots that is as permanent, and perhaps as timeless, as the ships themselves seem to be. So when I heard that *Texas* would be restored, I remembered what I had felt that day in 1977 in No. 3 turret. I knew I wanted some involvement with the ship, some part of this thing that, in happening, would tie time together, bring forward the past, and hold up a mirror to us that was worth the look.

One relative of mine says that reflection is not one he wants to see. But it is not Medusa's head that stares back at us; it is only ourselves. And if we move ahead at all, we humans, it will be because we looked behind, because we did not buy Satchel Paige's admonition not to look back, that something might be gaining on us. For only then, when time is snapping at our heels, do we surge ahead.

The finish line, of course, is nowhere in sight, and that itself is man's victory. Like the nuclear-tipped missiles of today, the dreadnought was to have been that finish, the final weapon, the ultimate arbiter of power. It didn't work. Man's life force was too great. And so *Texas* and all 177 other dreadnoughts are but signposts, offering equally guidance or deception, and only we can judge which we have found.

But there is this. A world in which there is no room for the artifacts of our past, peaceful or not, is not a world in which I want to live. For in the mirror the dreadnought offers, we find what we must know in order to survive: that we, and what we make, are part of something far greater than ourselves.

—HUGH POWER

Acknowledgments

No one makes a book alone. First-time authors like myself labor under the delusion that they do, but they are wrong. And only when authors sit down to compose the acknowledgments do they undergo the humbling realization of what a community effort their books really have been.

But it is well that it happens this way. The next book—and no one worth his advance check wants to stop at one—will go smoother for it.

In acknowledging all the helps, big and small, and quiet cheering that accompanied them down this path, authors may become better people for it. And if we can indulge the assumption that better people make better books, then the acknowledgments touch everyone who reads.

Like most authors, my list of benefactors is long. I do not even know the full names of some. But to all I am grateful. The list has no pecking order. All contributions were significant in their own way and moment. But it does seem right to start with those who took the raw fodder I offered and molded it into something of value.

I owe much to Noel Parsons, editor-in-chief at Texas A&M University Press. Horror tales about editors abound, but Noel banishes such nightmares. He does not do this with blue smoke and mirrors. He uses instead patience and tolerance and understanding and finally, on the close calls, the quiet firmness that salvages an author's product without banishing his ego to outer Mongolia. In short, if I could clone him, I would.

Noel's approach is supported by the entire A&M Press staff. They know how to make this whole book business seem less mystical and more possible, and they make you feel down home. To each of them I am grateful.

There would, of course, have been no book without the Texas Parks and Wildlife Department's dedication to what seemed impossible, the restoration of *Texas*. For that dedication and their support for an utterly unknown photographer, I want to thank Sue Moss, who ramrodded the restoration; Dr. Wilson E. Dolman, former director of the parks department; former *Texas* captain Frank Dengler, who helped with my technical comprehension; former captain Dan Harrison; and Orion Knox,

Strafford Morss, Bob Browning, Zane Morgan, Margarita Marders, Mary Cande, Jim Eaves, and Barry Hutcheson.

They were not isolated examples. Every Parks and Wildlife employee I encountered helped, from recovering mislaid equipment to finding light bulbs when I needed light. Each of them is a part of this book, and if it works, it works because of them.

For their technical support, I want to thank photographers Jim Cruz, who took two of the book's pictures, and Mike Luttrell; repair specialist Kerry Stamey and his associates at Houston Camera Repair, who kept my gear up and running; Paula Schutz and her fine crew at Skylark Camera Store in Clear Lake; and the staffs of the Ritz Camera Store in Galveston and Southwestern Camera in Houston. I also want to thank my earliest photography mentors: Bob Burns, former chief photographer of my hometown newspaper, the *Marshall News Messenger*; and Smith Kiker of the University of North Texas.

My thanks also to maritime artist Anthony Blackman of Gravesend, England, for simply cheering me on by letter and transatlantic call. We have never met, but he loves *Texas*, and his encouragement when it seemed the book might never find a publisher helped keep me going until it did.

I am especially indebted to the late Vaden Smith of Galveston, a long-time friend and frequent photography mentor. When pictures of *Texas* did not work, it was Vaden who offered suggestions and solved mysteries. Along the way he taught me to spot-tone, and he loaned me a 21mm lens, without which many of *Texas'* compartments could not have been photographed.

Sadly, Vaden did not live to see the book, but I believe he would have found it acceptable and been ready with suggestions to make the next one better. He was that kind of teacher, and I miss the man and his counsel.

I also want to thank Bob Grey, former head of Cordovan Publishing Company in Houston. He focused my thinking about marketing the book in a way that led me to Texas A&M. Bob cuts straight to the chase about marketing, which is something authors seldom can do for themselves. I recommend him to anyone trying a book, be it the first or fiftieth.

I could write volumes about those on the dedication page, but I don't have to. They know what I owe them, I know what I owe them, and we all know I'd have trouble just servicing the debt. To them I simply say thank you. You were there for me on this dream of mine, and an author knows how much that means only after the dream becomes a reality.

Battleship *Texas*

Introduction

J O H N   R E I L L Y

In American naval history, the name *Texas* goes back almost as far as Texas itself. Fittingly enough, the name is sometimes applied to the sailing sloop-of-war, more commonly referred to as *Austin*, built in Baltimore in 1839–40 for the Republic of Texas by order of Pres. Mirabeau Lamar. That ship flew Commodore Edwin Moore's flag during the naval battle of Campeche in 1843. *Austin/Texas* was turned over to the U.S. Navy when Texas entered the Union in 1846, but it was in such poor condition that it was soon broken up.

During the American Civil War two commercial steamers were taken over for Confederate service under the name *Texas*. One of them served on the western rivers as a transport and supply ship, and the other made successful runs through the Union blockade to Havana for arms, ammunition, and saltpeter for making gunpowder.

Three Confederate warships were named *Texas*, but none of them got into service. One, a steam sloop-of-war, was built at Nantes, France, in 1863, but the French government stepped in to prevent delivery. It was resold to Peru and served in that nation's navy as *America*. Another *Texas*, built in England, was intended to serve as a commerce raider like *Alabama*, which disrupted Union shipping. In this case both the American Federal and British governments kept the ship under such tight surveillance that the Confederates had to give up hope of getting it to sea. An ironclad ram, built at Richmond, was the last Confederate *Texas*. It was still incomplete when the Confederate capital fell in 1865. It was taken over by the U.S. Navy, but saw no active service. The unfinished hull was taken to Norfolk, where it was later sold. Confederates and Federals agreed that this ironclad, had it been finished in time, would have been a potent addition to the Confederate Navy.

The first USS *Texas*, like the subject of this book, was a battleship. It and the battleship *Maine* were commissioned in 1895 as the first capital ships of the new steel-hulled American navy of a century ago. These were our first pre-dreadnought battleships, as the type later came to be called—armored warships with a mixed offensive armament of heavy- and medium-caliber guns. This *Texas* was 309 feet long, about the size of a destroyer escort of World War II. Two turrets, each with one 12-inch gun (12 inches being the diameter of the bore), made up the main battery. The turrets were mounted in echelon, as the arrangement was called. One turret was mounted to port and the other to starboard in such a way that both guns could—at least theoretically—fire ahead and astern as well as to either beam. At that time the designers were still thinking about single-ship actions, in which the ship might have to generate maximum firepower in a chasing or withdrawing situation. These guns were backed up by six 6-inch guns along with smaller rapid-firing guns for defense against torpedo boats. *Texas* also had four torpedo tubes—widely used in battleships and cruisers at a time when effective combat gunnery range might be less than a mile.

The first USS *Texas* was built by the Norfolk Navy Yard and commissioned on August 15, 1895; it was the first American steel battleship to go into commission. The Spanish-American War was triggered by the mysterious explosion and sinking of *Maine* in Havana harbor early in 1898. *Texas* was assigned later that year to patrol and blockade duty off the southern coast of Cuba. The ship took a prominent part in the defeat of Spanish admiral Pascual Cervera's cruiser squadron in the naval battle of Santiago on July 3, 1898, and it made a triumphant return to New York soon afterward.

By that time *Texas'* armament and turret arrangement were already obsolete. The ship's successors were being built with four big guns instead of two, and the guns were mounted in twin turrets on the centerline. So its postwar service was fairly short. By 1908 it was being used as a station ship—in effect, a floating building—at Charleston, South Carolina. In 1911 the name was changed to *San Marcos* to let the name *Texas* be assigned to a new battleship, and later in that year it fulfilled its last duty as a gunnery target in the shallow waters of Chesapeake Bay. The riddled hulk yielded information on the effects of heavy gunfire on steel warship structures—information that would assist in the design of its descendants. The *San Marcos* Wreck, as it came to be called, was used for gunnery practice through World War II. Not until the late 1950s were the remains blasted far enough beneath the surface not to be a menace to passing bay traffic.

By the early 1900s the face of the navy was rapidly changing. *Texas* had been followed by several generations of battleships, completed between 1896 and 1908, called mixed-caliber ships. That is, like *Texas*, they carried 12- or 13-inch guns supported by medium-weight pieces, with quick-firers for close-in defense. Except for the first few, completed in time to take part in the Spanish-American War with *Texas*, the American pre-dreadnoughts never saw combat. Their position at the top of the naval heap was soon to be threatened.

In the early years of steel-ship navies, mixed-caliber capital ships made good sense. Early breech mechanisms for big guns took time to operate, giving them a slow rate of fire. Fire control—the science or, as some might say, the art of hitting a target—was crude to nonexistent. Ships had no centralized means of directing their fire; each gun and turret was individually aimed. At Santiago, *Texas'* captain had to designate targets by standing on top of his forward 12-inch gun turret and shouting through a hatch to the turret officer. Early steel guns, burning a form of black powder, were relatively short-barreled and threw their shells at low velocities. Longer ranges required higher trajectories, but accuracy tended to drop off, so effective shooting ranges were short—usually under a mile. Because the heaviest guns were inaccurate as well as slow-firing, they were assisted by batteries of medium-weight guns that threw lighter projectiles at a higher rate, making up in volume what they lacked in individual hitting power.

Early in the twentieth century a number of technical developments came together to revise this picture. Small-grain smokeless powders could produce higher pressures, and designers produced longer-barreled guns to accommodate them. New breech mechanisms enabled heavy guns to fire more rapidly. Projectiles were given better aerodynamic form, which helped accuracy and range. Soft metal caps, placed over the noses of armor-piercing shells, prestressed any armor plating that they hit. This permitted the hardened body of the shell to drive into the plate more effectively. Optical rangefinders and electrical devices to transmit orders and information, with simple analog computers to combine the many elements involved in aiming a heavy gun at long range, were also added. These let a ship's guns be aimed from a central station, firing together at the same bearing and elevation at the same target.

Spurred by gunnery reformers, new training methods were devised to take advantage of the new technology. Gunnery competition pitted ship against ship and stimulated a spirit of excellence. As torpedoes gradually improved in speed and range, fighting at the old close-in ranges became increasingly dangerous, and longer-ranged gunnery became a tactical necessity. As ranges grew, the utility of medium-caliber guns lessened. Designers and naval officers began to look at completely doing away with them in favor of the improved heavy guns, which had attained the ability to fire more rapidly and accurately at greater ranges.

The first ship to embody this new concept was the British battleship *Dreadnought*, completed in 1906. Whereas a typical battleship had carried four 12-inch guns and an array of medium pieces, *Dreadnought* was armed with ten 12-inch guns. The British ship was a catalyst in its time and spurred the other major navies to produce all-big-gun designs of their own. In the United States, this process crystallized in the *South Carolina* class, two battleships authorized by Congress in 1905. The designers had been looking at a number of all-big-gun and mixed-caliber concepts for the new ships, but *Dreadnought* settled the matter. The *South Carolina*s were laid down in 1906 as the first U.S. dreadnought battleships, carrying eight 12-inch guns in four centerline turrets arranged in stepped, or "superfiring," positions forward and aft. Class followed class in fairly quick succession as the U.S. Navy, strongly supported by Pres. Theodore Roosevelt, sought to build up its all-big-gun battle force. The *Delaware*-class ships were large enough to take five 12-inch twin turrets; the *Florida* class mounted the same main battery. And in 1909 Congress authorized *Wyoming* and *Arkansas*, bigger still than their forerunners and carrying twelve 12-inch guns in six twin turrets. As long as 12-inch guns and two-gun turrets were the best the United States could produce, that was as far as the designers could go.

Late in 1908, however, when the design for the *Wyoming* class was approved, work was ordered on a new 14-inch gun, which had been under consideration for some time. American naval leaders believed that foreign navies, previously using 11- or 12-inch guns, would soon adopt heavier ones; Britain was already working on a 13.5-incher. In the spring of 1909 the navy's General Board—the committee of senior officers responsible for advising the secretary of the navy and, among other things, shaping the designs of new ships—started to look at the ships that would follow the *Wyoming*s. The 14-inch gun was still being developed, so the board sketched an improved *Wyoming* mounting the new 14-incher as well as a similar ship with a 12-inch battery. In early 1910 the 14-inch gun was test-fired, and the testers praised its accuracy. This settled the question of armament, and Battleships Nos. 34 and 35, funded by Congress on June 24, 1910, were ordered as the first 14-inch-gun capital ships for the U.S. Navy. These were, in fact, the first 14-inch guns in any navy at the time. (The more familiar "BB" designation for battleships did not appear until 1920.)

Sketch designs for the new battleships were debated for some months. Armor protection, hull form, and power plant were considered. The final design was worked out by the fall of 1910. Battleship No. 34 was ordered from the New York Navy Yard. Number 35 was to be built at a commercial shipyard, and a tender for bids went out on September 27. The contract was awarded to the Newport News Shipbuilding and Drydock Company of Virginia. By this time the secretary of the navy had

Fig. 1. This photograph, taken soon after *Texas'* commissioning in 1914, shows only part of the total ship's company of 1,052 officers and men. Capt. Albert W. Grant, the first captain of *Texas,* appears immediately above and behind the life ring. *Courtesy Texas Parks and Wildlife Department*

named Battleship No. 34 *New York,* and No. 35 became *Texas.* The new *Texas* was laid down on April 17, 1911. On May 18, 1912, Claudia Lyon—young daughter of Cecil A. Lyon, a Republican national committee member from Texas—broke the traditional champagne bottle across the unfinished hull's bow, and the ship went down the builder's ways. Miss Mary Colquitt, daughter of Texas governor Oscar B. Colquitt, was one of the maids of honor. Fifteen thousand spectators saw *Texas* enter the water for the first time as a movie camera took what were thought to be the first motion pictures of the launching of a U.S. Navy ship.

At the time of the launching much remained to be done before *Texas* would be ready to go to sea. Machinery and armament had to be installed, and the superstructure and upperworks were still to be fabricated. But in less than two years the ship

Fig. 2. The first commander of *Texas*, from commissioning on March 12, 1914, to June 10, 1915, was Capt. Albert Weston Grant, shown here two years later as vice admiral in command of a division of the fleet. *Courtesy Texas Parks and Wildlife Department*

was completed, and builder's trials took it into the Atlantic to see if it would steam and steer according to contract. On March 12, 1914, *Texas* was commissioned into service, and Capt. Albert W. Grant assumed command.

The new battleship measured 573 feet in length and a bit over 95 feet in the beam, with a designed displacement of 27,000 tons. It was simple and uncluttered in appearance. A large deck-house forward housed captain's quarters and offices, chart house, bridge, and conning tower—the armored cylinder from which the ship was supposed to be commanded in battle. A cage foremast, made of interwoven steel tubing, held searchlight platforms, radio wires, and signal yardarms, with a small platform at the top for the main-battery rangefinders and for spotting gunfire. Further aft, smaller deckhouses held galleys and workshops; the aftermost of these supported the cage mainmast. Five turrets each held a pair of 14-inch guns. Two pairs of turrets were superimposed forward and aft. The fifth turret had to be placed between the engine room and the boiler rooms in order to distribute the massive weight of the turrets more evenly along the box girder that made up the ship's hull. Unfortunately, that location made it necessary to run steam pipes around the midships magazines to bring power to the engines. This, in turn, caused temperature problems in those magazines in spite of insulation and a cool-air circulating system.

For defense against destroyer attack, *Texas* carried eighteen 5-inch rapid-fire guns in casemates—gun compartments in the sides of the hull just below the main deck—two more up on the forward bridge deck, and one in the very stern of the ship. Four torpedo tubes were installed forward, below the waterline, two tubes on each side. Antiaircraft guns were conspicuously absent. At that time the military airplane was still an infant, and antiaircraft guns would not begin to appear in American battleships until 1916.

Texas' scheme of protection was typical of that built into American battleships of that generation. The waterline was shielded by what was called belt armor. This was a connected series of face-hardened carbon steel plates nearly 8 feet wide and 12 inches thick at the top, tapering below the waterline to 10 inches at the bottom. The hull sides above the belt carried casemate armor, 11 inches thick at the bottom and 9 inches thick at the top. The uppermost hull deck, where the 5-inch guns were mounted, was protected by 6.5-inch armor. Bulkheads with 1-inch armor separated the 5-inch gun compartments, and 1.5-inch bulkheads ran fore and aft behind the gun compartments on either side. The protective deck, just above the waterline, had 1 inch of armor forward of the turrets, 1.5 inches amidships, and 2.5 inches aft, sloping downward to protect the vital propeller shafts and steering gear. Gun turrets had 14-inch-thick faceplates, with sides 8–9 inches thick and 4 inches of armor on their roofs. The cylindrical barbettes that protected ammunition hoists and turret machinery ranged from 12 to 5 inches thick. The conning tower's sides were 12 inches thick, and its roof was 4 inches thick.

Texas' underwater protection was like that of the *Wyoming* class. A double bottom ran from the keel past the waterline to the protective deck. Just inboard to either side was a torpedo-

Fig. 3. The members of a 5-inch gun crew clown around during gun drill aboard *Texas*, probably sometime before World War I. This gun, mounted on the starboard forward superstructure deck, and its mate on the port side were later replaced by antiaircraft guns. The device mounted atop the large gun barrel was a small-caliber gun that was fired in practice to conserve large-bore ammunition. *Courtesy Texas Parks and Wildlife Department*

defense bulkhead made of light armor to protect the magazines and engine rooms. Also behind this bulkhead, along the boiler rooms, was a row of coal bunkers; the coal formed an additional layer of protection. The outer void compartments on both sides were cross-connected by valveless equalizing pipes that were intended to automatically flood the compartment opposite any damaged one to keep the ship on a more or less even keel. This sounded good in theory but did not work well in practice, so eventually the equalizing pipes were shut off.

Fourteen coal-burning Babcock and Wilcox boilers, arranged in four watertight firerooms, generated steam at a working pressure of 295 pounds per square inch; eight of the boilers had superheaters. *Texas* and *New York* were the last American capital ships to use coal for fuel, and even their boilers were fitted with auxiliary burners to use oil for supplementary power if needed.

When Battleship No. 35 was advertised for bidding, the specification called for turbines but allowed bidders to propose high-performance reciprocating piston engines instead. When Newport News offered to use reciprocating engines, the bid was accepted for good reason. Early experience with turbines in battleships and cruisers had shown that turbines were heavy burners of coal, giving their ships relatively short range. But American battleships had to be capable of high steaming endurance to cover the distances required by the strategic thinking of the time. This requirement for long range dictated what seemed to be a step backward. *Texas* was built with a pair of vertical, 4-cylinder, triple-expansion reciprocating engines generating 28,100 horsepower to turn two three-bladed, 18⅔-foot-diameter propellers. The engines were fitted with a forced lubrication system that circulated oil to nearly all of their working parts. This made them considerably more reliable at higher speeds than earlier engines of this kind, which had been annoyingly prone to break down. *Texas'* construction contract called for the ship to make 21 knots (nautical miles per hour) in a four-hour speed trial and 19 knots in a twenty-four-hour endurance trial. It met and slightly exceeded both speeds.

After the initial tests, fire-control gear was installed on the newly commissioned battleship at New York Navy Yard. It was then scheduled for the usual shakedown cruise. This period of tests and training gets a crew accustomed to its ship and looks for flaws that will then be corrected during a post-shakedown period in a shipyard. Instead, *Texas* had to forego shakedown and headed for the Gulf of Mexico to take part in President Wilson's naval intervention at Veracruz, Mexico. After two months at Veracruz, it returned to New York for two weeks' overhaul before going back to Mexico for brief periods of service at Tuxpan and Tampico. By the end of 1914 it had returned to New York.

In 1915 *Texas* finally began normal fleet operations off the East Coast. Training exercises took place off New England and in the Southern Drill Grounds, an area off the entrance to Hampton Roads, Virginia. During the winter months the fleet moved to the Caribbean for tactical exercises and gunnery shoots.

Peacetime routine was interrupted when the United States entered World War I in April, 1917. *Texas* was in the southern end of Chesapeake Bay, at the mouth of the York River just north of Norfolk. It remained in this general area through the summer, helping train the large number of Naval Armed Guard gun crews suddenly needed to arm American merchant ships and troop transports. One of these gun crews, drafted from *Texas'* crew, was assigned to the merchant vessel *Mongolia* at the beginning of the war. On the way from the United States to England on April 19, 1917, the ship's lookouts sighted a surfaced German submarine. The gun crew manned a 6-inch gun on *Mongolia*'s stern platform and opened fire, averting a possible attack. Thus it can be said that *Texas* had, albeit indirectly, helped fire the first American shots of World War I. *Mongolia*'s 6-inch gun stood outside the Smithsonian Institution for many years; it is now at the Washington Navy Yard.

In late 1917 *Texas* went to New York for overhaul. After the overhaul, while steaming around Long Island headed for Port Jefferson, New York, it ran aground off Block Island in the early hours of September 27, 1917. As tugs helped free it three days later, shouts of "Come on, *Texas*" from onlookers gave the ship a motto. Damage to the underwater hull was serious enough to require repair at New York. *Texas* was to have gone to England with its unit—Battleship Division 9—in November, but the division had to sail without it. Hull repairs were finished a month later, and *Texas* returned to Chesapeake Bay for tactical exercises.

In January of 1918, *Texas* went to New York to prepare for the voyage to Britain. It sailed from New York on January 30 and on February 11 rejoined Division 9 at the British Grand Fleet's base at Scapa Flow, in the Orkney Islands north of Scotland. The division was now operating with the Grand Fleet. In the British organization, it was known as the 6th Battle Squadron.

By that time no major surface-fleet combat was taking place in those waters. *Texas*' service was demanding, involving sorties from Scapa Flow and from the Firth of Forth to operate with British battleships in the North Sea and to protect troop convoys from possible attack. Its closest approach to combat came on April 24, 1918, when the division put to sea to intercept the German High Seas Fleet, which was heading northward across the North Sea to attack an Allied convoy. Although screening ships sighted each other, the Germans withdrew to their base before shots could be fired. Then for several days in midsummer, *Texas* and the other American battleships covered minelayers planting enormous minefields. Called the North Sea Mine Barrage, it was designed to close the north end of that body of water to passage by submarines.

Experience at sea led to the removal of *Texas*' four hull-mounted forward 5-inch guns and the single gun mounted in the extreme stern. It was also found that the open navigating bridge was hardly suited to work in the North Sea, so a closed wheelhouse replaced it.

Armistice ended World War I combat on November 11, 1918. Under the terms of the armistice, the German fleet was to be

Fig. 4. Late in 1917, *Texas'* hull was damaged when it ran aground off Block Island, outside New York Harbor. Here the ship is being hauled into position in the Brooklyn Navy Yard drydock for repairs. *Courtesy Texas Parks and Wildlife Department*

interned at Scapa Flow while the terms of the final peace treaty were negotiated. On November 21, *Texas* was with the British and American warships that rendezvoused with the German fleet in the North Sea and escorted it into Scapa Flow. In mid-December *Texas* was with the battleships that got underway from England to meet President Wilson, who was in the troopship *George Washington*. They escorted him into Brest, France,

Fig. 5. While *Texas* was in drydock for repairs in 1917, the navy took the opportunity to clean and repaint the battleship's hull. Note the original curve of the hull, before the addition of the anti-torpedo bulge, and the openings of the torpedo tubes just above the scaffold near the center of the picture. *Courtesy Texas Parks and Wildlife Department*

on his way to the Versailles Peace Conference. Their mission done, the ships headed for the United States. The battleships entered New York harbor on the day after Christmas, and sailors and Marines from the ships paraded through Manhattan.

Texas returned to peacetime service, which included trying out new military techniques and equipment. Navies had been, for some time, trying to devise satisfactory means of taking airplanes to sea. During World War I the British tried launching land planes from flying-off platforms, which were miniature runways mounted on top of gun turrets. The platform was rigged extending from the top of the turret out to the muzzles of its guns, and the turret was trained into the wind. The plane, held in place by a line attached to a quick-release pelican hook, revved its engine to full power. Then the pelican hook was

Fig. 6. This Sopwith biplane was the first aircraft to be launched from a U.S. ship when it was successfully flown from the platform mounted on top of No. 2 turret in March, 1919. *Courtesy National Archives*

tripped, the plane ran down the platform, and, if all went well, it took off. This plan was not as ludicrous as it sounds today; early airplanes were light enough to do such things.

On March 9, 1919, *Texas* tested a flying-off platform when Lt. Comdr. Edward O. McDonnell took off from the ship in a British Sopwith Camel fighter. The experiment worked. Until catapults were installed in battleships, they carried turret platforms and operated such World War I aircraft as Sopwith Camels and 1½-Strutters, Hanriot HD.1s, and Nieuport 28s.

In May, 1919, *Texas* took station with other battleships and a chain of destroyers. They were guarding the way from Newfoundland to the Azores for the navy's attempt to fly seaplanes

Fig. 7. *Texas*, along with other ships of the U.S. Fleet, passes through Gatun Lake in the Panama Canal on July 25, 1919, on the way to the Pacific. The battleship in the midview on the left may be *New York*, a ship of the same class as *Texas*. Note the gun tracking dial painted around *Texas'* No. 4 turret and the ranging "clock" mounted on the mast. Before the days of reliable ship-to-ship radio communication, these dials helped battleships direct their fire at the same target on which another ship was firing, even though smoke might obscure the target. *Courtesy National Archives*

across the Atlantic. The battleships took weather observations and broadcast them. To keep planes on course, the destroyers made smoke during the day and marked the planes' path with searchlights and star shells by night. During the flight, one of the seaplanes, NC-3, was reported down at sea, and *Texas* joined in the search for it, only to find that the plane had taxied the last 35 miles across the water to safety in the Azores. Another

16

of the flight, NC-4, completed the entire course and arrived in England, demonstrating that aircraft could cross the ocean and adding honor to the new naval air service.

During the summer of 1919 *Texas* passed through the Panama Canal to report for duty with the Pacific Fleet. On July 17, 1920, the numerical identification Battleship No. 35 was replaced by the more familiar designation BB35 by order of the secretary of the navy. *Texas* remained in the Pacific until 1924, but it returned to Atlantic waters in the summer of that year to take Naval Academy midshipmen on their annual training cruise to European waters. By that time the Atlantic and Pacific fleets had been merged to form the United States Fleet, subdivided by task into a Battle Fleet and a Scouting Fleet (renamed Battle Force and Scouting Force in 1931). *Texas* was assigned to the Scouting Fleet, with which it would serve for the next six years.

Although the battleships' guns had fallen silent with the armistice, the years following World War I were still a period of international political activity that would continue to affect the navies. The Washington Treaty, signed in 1922, was an attempt by the major naval powers to head off a naval arms race among Britain, Japan, and the United States. France and Italy joined in that agreement, which capped the various nations' battleship strengths in numbers, individual ship size (35,000 tons), and gun caliber (16 inches). The nations also agreed on a ten-year building holiday. Because new ships could not be built, the treaty permitted navies to modernize their existing battleships, adding up to 3,000 tons "for providing means of defense against air and submarine attack."

In the United States, Congress appropriated funds for the modernization process, and work began on the battleship force. The oldest coal burners were taken in hand first. The *Florida* and *Wyoming* classes received relatively moderate upgradings, including conversion of their boilers to use oil fuel. *New York* and *Texas* followed, entering the shipyards in 1925. *Texas* went to the Norfolk Navy Yard, and there its appearance was considerably altered. Six new oil-burning boilers were trunked into a single stack. The cage foremast was removed to make way for an enlarged forward superstructure and a tripod mast. This mast was better able to carry the massive weight of modern fire control equipment for the 14-inch guns as well as the 5-inch directors, which now moved into the fire control tops from positions on deck.

The cage mainmast was also replaced by a tripod, but the ship's size would not allow it to carry another heavy fire control top at any elevation. Yet battleship commanders, thinking in terms of long-range surface gunnery, wanted the redundancy of a second control top, even if it could not be carried aloft.

Fig. 8. *Texas* leads a column of battleships in gunnery exercises in the Pacific in 1921. *Courtesy U.S. Navy*

Therefore, in *Texas* and *New York* the mainmast was given over to searchlights, and the after fire control top was mounted in a truss tower located amidships. This location was not ideal, but it was feasible in terms of stability. In addition, it did not interfere with the new airplane catapult, which was mounted on top of the midship turret for lack of better location.

Texas' hull-mounted 5-inch gun positions amidships—like the forward gun positions, which had been removed during World War I—had proven to take on water in anything short of a calm sea. Because of this, during the 1925 refitting most of these guns were moved up to the main deck into sponsons built out from the ship's sides to give a good field of fire and to keep the guns drier. Two more pairs of guns remained in hull casemates amidships, with another two pairs in the hull toward the stern. Another pair of guns remained on the superstructure deck. By that

Fig. 9. Stern view of *Texas* in drydock in Norfolk, Virginia, May 7, 1925. Work on the ship at this point seems to be mainly internal. The torpedo blisters and gun sponsons have not yet been added, and the cage masts have not yet been replaced by tripods. This major modernization of the ship was completed in the summer of 1927. *Courtesy National Archives*

time a 5-inch antiaircraft gun had been developed for battle-ships, but the perennial shortage of funds gave priority to newer ships. *Texas* kept its battery of eight 3-inch antiaircraft guns grouped amidships above the 5-inch sponsons.

A lengthy series of explosive tests against models and full-sized mockups of battleship torpedo-protection systems had shown the need for additional layers of watertight compartmentation. This would permit capital ships to survive hits by the

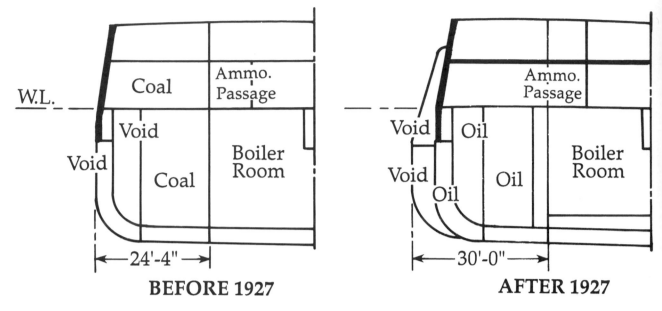

W.L.

Coal

Ammo.
Passage

Void

Boiler
Room

Void

Coal

←——24'-4"——→

BEFORE 1927

Void | Oil

Ammo.
Passage

Void

Boiler
Room

Oil

Oil

←——30'-0"——→

AFTER 1927

Fig. 10. Changes in *Texas'* torpedo protection system during the 1925–27 modernization are shown by these drawings, which are based on a contemporary manual. The void spaces and oil tanks after the refitting were calculated to give protection as good as, or better than, the original voids backed by coal bunkers. In addition, armor was added to deck 2 amidships to protect vital machinery spaces against bombs. *Courtesy U.S. Navy*

more powerful torpedo warheads that had been developed. There was not enough room to add these compartments within the hulls of the older ships, such as *Texas.* Instead, blisters—external additions to the underwater hull—were added. The blisters also provided the buoyancy needed to carry the added weight of modernization at the original designed waterline, thus keeping the waterline armor belt in proper position to protect against hits. *Texas'* overall beam was restricted to 106 feet by the width of the Panama Canal, so the battleship's blisters added only five feet to either beam.

Torpedo tubes on battleships had long since been considered useless, and the large torpedo rooms were liabilities for damage control, so *Texas'* tubes were removed during the modernization, and the spaces were subdivided into smaller compartments.

Also during the refitting, an additional internal bulkhead of nickel steel was added outboard of the innermost bulkhead that protected the machinery spaces. This provided five successive layers of protection. Here again, this was hardly ideal, but it was feasible. Horizontal armor plate, originally made for the battleships and battlecruisers canceled by the Washington Treaty, was added between the forward and after turrets to protect magazines and engineering spaces from bombs and high-trajectory, long-range shell hits.

Texas' blisters and added weight did not affect its handling at higher speeds. They did, however, hamper the ship somewhat at lower cruising speeds, and they affected its stability. The ship was "stiff" and did not roll much in rough seas, but this stiffness had its drawbacks. It made the ship roll heavily and erratically while at anchor in open waters or in swells from either quarter—not the most desirable quality for a ship designed to fire its guns accurately.

Texas emerged from the modernization in 1927 as flagship of the commander in chief, United States Fleet, and proceeded to San Diego via the Panama Canal. Thereafter, *Texas* alternated periods of service in the Pacific and Atlantic. In 1928 it carried Pres. Calvin Coolidge to Havana, Cuba, for a Pan-American conference, then it returned to the West Coast to take part in the annual Fleet Problem. This was a month or so of large-scale fleet strategic and tactical war games, a seagoing laboratory in which concepts of operating doctrine were tested. More service in both oceans followed. After an overhaul at New York in 1931 it returned to San Diego, and during the six years that followed, it operated as flagship of Battleship Division 1. In 1937 *Texas* returned to the East Coast as flagship of the Training Detachment, United States Fleet, and later it became flagship of the newly created Atlantic Squadron.

On the East Coast, *Texas* once again became the platform for the testing of new naval equipment—this time a new development in electronics. Since 1922 the navy had looked into the idea of detecting and locating objects by reflected radio waves. Through the 1920s and 1930s the project slowly approached reality. Engineers looked at the possibilities of blind navigation, detection of contacts in darkness or fog, and spotting gunfire by high-frequency radio detection. A crude prototype was tested by the destroyer *Leary* in 1937, and by 1938 the chief of naval operations was ready to ask that an experimental radio detection set be sent to sea for trials with the fleet. The Naval Research Laboratory built 200-megahertz (mHz) equipment, designated XAF, and the Radio Corporation of American (RCA) was given a contract to develop a 400-megahertz set, designated CXZ by the navy.

By the end of 1938 both sets were ready. The XAF was mounted in *New York*, and *Texas* got the CXZ. In the early months of 1939 both ships gave their equipment a thorough tryout in fleet exercises and gunnery shoots. *New York*'s XAF turned out to be the better of the two. The commander of the Atlantic Squadron reported that it was "one of the most important military developments since the advent of radio itself" and recommended that it be fitted to all larger warships. While *Texas'* commanding officer judged the CXZ of little value as it then was, he advised the navy to continue to stimulate commercial

Fig. 11. After a 1931 overhaul, *Texas* moored in New York City for a short time before returning to the Pacific for additional duty as flagship of the United States Fleet. The flag bridge appears here for the first time. *Courtesy National Archives*

development by RCA. This test by the two identical battleships gave the navy what it would later call radar. Before 1939 was out, a production contract for "radio range equipment" would be awarded, and the first service radars would be installed in warships during 1940. *Texas* had helped bring about something that would, sooner than anyone realized, be seen as a revolution in naval warfare.

World War II broke out in Europe in September of 1939. *Texas* was soon assigned to the Neutrality Patrol, which was established by order of Pres. Franklin Roosevelt to protect the shipping of the United States and other neutral countries. *Texas* patrolled the grim waters of the North Atlantic as the war grew in scope and intensity and as the United States came closer to active support of Britain and its allies. On June 20, 1941, *Texas* was put at hazard when the patrolling German submarine *U-203* sighted it on station west of Greenland. The U-boat captain assumed that *Texas* had been transferred to England and spent hours attempting to get into attack position. Submerged submarines of that day could make no more than a few knots, however, and *Texas'* speed and zigzag course kept the U-boat from succeeding.

When the bombing of Pearl Harbor brought the United States into the war, *Texas* was at Casco Bay, Maine. It carried out more North Atlantic patrols, took station at Iceland in case of a threatened sortie by the German battleship *Tirpitz* from Norway, and escorted troop convoys to the Panama Canal, West Africa, and Scotland. During 1942 radar and modern light antiaircraft guns began to be added to the ship's outfit. As equipment and scheduling permitted, air- and surface-search radars were installed. Batteries of 40mm and 20mm automatic guns appeared and grew to supplement the 3-inch antiaircraft guns. By the end of World War II *Texas* mounted ten four-barreled 40mm mounts and forty-four 20mm guns. Fire control for the smaller guns was relatively primitive, but those weapons gave *Texas* the ability to throw up an amount of automatic shell fire that was serviceable for its time.

Late in August of 1942 Texas was assigned to the naval task force that would carry American troops from Hampton Roads to take part in Operation Torch, the Allied landings in North Africa. On October 23, 1942, *Texas* sailed with the task force as flagship of the attack group aimed at Mehedia and Port Lyautey, Morocco. During the night of November 7 it arrived off Mehedia. The battleship's big guns were silent; at this early stage of the war, army planners did not recognize any role for gunfire before the landing. They insisted on landing in darkness without preliminary bombardment in the hope of achieving tactical surprise. Not until the afternoon of November 8 did *Texas* join the fight, hitting an ammunition dump outside Port Lyautey.

Through the next week *Texas* gave fire support to the landing forces as requested. On November 10 the ship struck Vichy (German-allied) French reinforcement convoys. During that afternoon its observation floatplanes attacked French tanks and troops approaching Port Lyautey for a counterattack, strafing and dropping a depth charge with an instantaneous fuse on a tank. *Texas* also sent a landing party ashore for temporary duty to organize the shipping that was arriving at Port Lyautey to unload supplies. A cease-fire was arranged with the Vichy government of Morocco on November 11, and some of *Texas'* crew helped salvage sunken ships and unload military cargo to support the American forces in their push toward Algeria.

On the night of November 12, *Texas* was on station off the coast when screening destroyers began dropping depth charges on a suspected U-boat contact. The battleship ran evasive maneuvers until things cleared up, then the next day it landed war correspondent Walter Cronkite at Port Lyautey. *Texas* returned to Norfolk on November 26.

During 1943 *Texas* served as flagship of the escort forces for three large troop and supply convoys from the United States to North Africa while Allied forces mastered that area and landed in Sicily and Italy. In the fall and winter it protected two similar convoys taking American troops and war materiel to Britain in preparation for the planned landing in France. After an early 1944 overhaul at Boston, the ship went to Casco Bay for training. Early in April *Texas* sailed from New York with a convoy for Scotland and then went on to Belfast Lough, Northern Ireland, for the installation of electronic jamming gear and equipment to be used with the new Loran radio navigation system.

Training and preparation went on apace as troops and supplies massed in seemingly endless numbers under the tightest security. On May 19, 1944, Gen. Dwight Eisenhower, supreme commander of the Allied Expeditionary Force, visited *Texas* to speak to the crew. Final decisions were made, and the invasion was given the signal to go. Through the night of June 5, 1944, thousands of landing craft and supporting ships streamed across the English Channel toward the coast of Normandy. In the early hours of D-Day, June 6, *Texas* took its station as the flagship of the Omaha Beach bombardment group. The army had learned something about landing operations since North Africa, but not enough. The commander of the naval task force had asked for two hours of bombardment before the first wave went ashore, but army commanders successfully argued for only forty minutes of fire, saying that two hours would give the Germans time to bring up reinforcements. Bombardment knocked out about half of the artillery defending Omaha, but the landing troops were still met with heavy fire as they tried to fight their way through shallow-water obstacles, minefields, a seawall and steep bluffs, and beach fortifications armed with mortars, machine guns, and light artillery. In spite of severe losses, the Americans and British got onto the beaches, held their ground, and slowly began to push inland.

What got them through was heavy, accurate gunfire from *Texas* and *Arkansas*, along with British and French cruisers and a dozen destroyers. Rear Adm. Carleton Bryant, commander of the naval gunfire force, called all the fire support ships over his

Fig. 12. In 1943 *Texas* was working with the U.S. Coast Guard as a convoy escort for troopships and transports headed to England in preparation for the invasion of Normandy. The ship's colors at that time were Camouflage Measure 22: gray on the upper hull and vertical surfaces of the superstructure and dark blue on the lower hull and horizontal surfaces, with dark stripes painted along the upper surfaces of the big guns to match them with the dark blue decks. *Courtesy National Archives*

voice radio: "Get on them, men! Get on them! They're raising Hell with the men on the beach, and we can't have any more of that. We must stop it!" The bombardment ships responded magnificently. Battleships and cruisers created a ring of fire around the beachhead, cutting the defenders off from reinforcements. Ernest Hemingway told of soldiers in a landing craft

Fig. 13. On the bridge of *Texas* during the bombardment of the German defensive lines at Normandy on June 6, 1944. *Left to right:* Cecil Carnes, correspondent for the *Saturday Evening Post*; Rear Adm. Carleton Bryant, commander of naval gunfire; 1st Lt. Weldon James, USMC; and Capt. C. A. Baker, commander of *Texas. Courtesy National Archives*

"watching the *Texas* with looks of surprise and happiness. Under their steel helmets they looked like pikemen of the Middle Ages, to whose aid in battle had suddenly come some strange and unbelievable monster." Destroyers closed the beach, some touching bottom, to hit targets of opportunity or give fire support at the call of naval gunfire spotters with the landing troops. By that evening casualties among the landing forces had added up, but most of two divisions were ashore, and Omaha Beach-

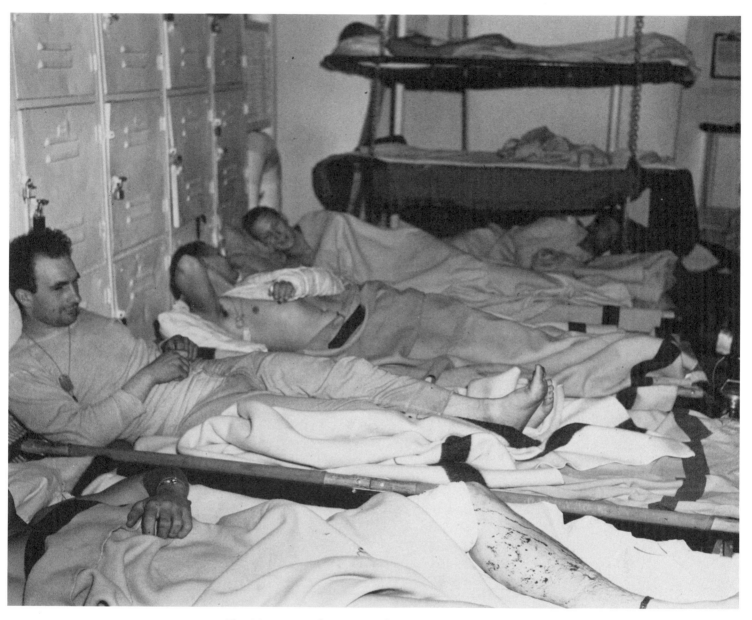

Fig. 14. During the Normandy invasion *Texas* took on wounded soldiers for transport to hospitals in England. Here, U.S. Army Rangers from the battle for Pointe du Hoc rest after treatment in a temporary dressing station set up in the crew's area. *Courtesy National Archives*

head was a going concern. The army's 1st Infantry Division put it tersely in its report: "Without that gunfire, we positively could not have crossed the beaches."

On June 7, *Texas* continued, hitting targets inshore and sending food and ammunition ashore to Rangers isolated at Pointe du Hoc. The ship remained off the beachhead until June 9, then moved back to England for two days to take on supplies and ammunition. On June 15 it bombarded strong points

Fig. 15. A fountain of water thrown up by the near miss of an exploding German shell towers nearly as high as the mast tops of *Texas* during its duel with shore batteries at Cherbourg, France, on June 25, 1944. *Courtesy U.S. Navy*

on high ground between the Norman towns of Isigny and Carentan at the request of army troops. The range was over twenty thousand yards (11.4 miles), so Capt. Charles Baker, *Texas'* commanding officer, gave the ship's guns a needed two more degrees of elevation by flooding the starboard blisters and giving the ship a list. *Texas* returned to England on June 18, carrying the commendation of Adm. John Hall, Jr., commander of the Omaha Beach amphibious force, who called the ship's fire support "invaluable."

Texas headed back for France on June 25 with *Arkansas* and three destroyers. By this time the VII Corps was pushing out from the original beachhead into the Cotentin Peninsula, capped at its northern end by the port city of Cherbourg. The French had fortified Cherbourg before World War II, and the Germans had strengthened its defenses during the occupation. One of its strongest points was Battery Hamburg, a complex containing four 280mm (11-inch) guns and protected by heavy, medium, and light antiaircraft guns. Shortly after noon, as the bombardment ships approached Cherbourg and began firing, Battery Hamburg returned their fire. Salvos straddled one of the screening destroyers and a nearby minesweeper, and one round landed ahead of *Texas*. Battery Hamburg's third salvo straddled *Texas'* bow, and the ship came hard to starboard just as another salvo missed its stern.

The destroyers laid a smoke screen, and *Texas* dodged

Fig. 16. *Texas* sustained its heaviest damage during the exchange with German shore batteries at Cherbourg when a large shell hit the armored conning tower and exploded under the navigation bridge. This photograph shows the damage to the floor of the bridge. The base of the helm, the ship's main steering wheel, can be seen at the top of the picture. *Courtesy National Archives*

through it to close the coastline. The ship emerged from the smoke and was again taken under fire. Within minutes a German shell struck the top of the armored conning tower and exploded, demolishing *Texas'* bridge, killing the helmsman, and wounding eleven other men. Captain Baker was knocked from his feet but escaped injury. He quickly cleared everyone from

Fig. 17. The crew of a 3-inch antiaircraft gun goes through loading drills on the afterdeck of *Texas. Courtesy U.S. Navy*

the bridge, and the ship's executive officer continued to handle the ship from the conning tower. The battleships continued their duel with the coastal battery, during which *Texas* evaded more than sixty-five straddles and near misses. The ships were ordered to retire at 3:00 P.M., but a few minutes before that a 240mm (9.4-inch) armor-piercing shell from another of Cherbourg's guns was discovered in one of the forward living spaces. It had apparently hit *Texas* near the port bow but had failed to explode. Since no one was stationed in that area, no one had noticed when it hit.

Texas received full credit for the work off Cherbourg. Admiral Bryant reported that the battleship's performance, "while under heavy and accurate fire of the enemy, was outstanding. She was smartly handled and continued the engagement until ordered to withdraw, although hopelessly outranged and continuously harassed by enemy fire over a period of two hours and twenty minutes." Army commanders also praised the quality of the ship's bombardment. Maj. Gen. J. Lawton Collins, commander of the VII Corps, credited the success of his troops "in a great measure to the fine support given . . . by the gunfire of your naval forces on D-Day and thereafter."

Battle damage was soon repaired, and *Texas* sailed from Belfast in mid-July to support the landings in southern France. It arrived off Saint-Tropez during the night of August 14, 1944. Early the next morning, it joined the battleship *Nevada*, the cruiser *Philadelphia*, and French cruisers and destroyers in pounding the center portion of the objective area. These beaches were fortified, and trouble had been expected. During an hour and a half of prelanding bombardment, the ships closed to within three thousand yards as they hammered their targets. The expected opposition did not materialize; heavy air attack and naval gunfire killed the defenders or drove them from their positions, and the landing went in unopposed. Troops moved inland against no more than light resistance, helped by the steady support of the warships. By the evening of August 16, 1944, *Texas* left the area and set course for New York.

After a month of overhaul, including regunning of the 14-inch turrets, *Texas* headed for duty in the Pacific. After a pause at Long Beach, California, the ship arrived at Pearl Harbor in early December for training exercises, including bombardment firings. From Hawaii it moved to Ulithi, in the Caroline Islands, early in January of 1945. And after landing rehearsals in the Marianas, it arrived off Japanese-held Iwo Jima early on the morning of February 16 and immediately participated in the prelanding bombardment of that island.

Task Force 54—the gunfire force that included *Texas* and five other battleships, five cruisers, and sixteen destroyers—continued to hit Japanese defenses through the two following days. During the afternoon of February 18 one of *Texas*' seaplanes rescued a Marine fighter pilot shot down at sea.

The Marines went ashore on the morning of February 19. Bombardment and air strikes had pounded the island heavily, but the Japanese were carefully dug in, and the landing met strong opposition. Every foot had to be fought for, and the island was not declared secured until March 16. Fighting went on for another ten days. *Texas* remained off Iwo Jima until March 7, providing fire in support of the ground troops. In his last radio report before the fall of the island, the Japanese commander re-

Fig. 18. Somewhere in the Pacific early in 1945, members of one of *Texas'* 40mm gun crews stand by their battle stations, with spotters alert for the approach of Japanese aircraft. The positions and duties of the crew are shown in the accompanying drawing, from a wartime manual. *Photograph courtesy National Archives, drawing courtesy U.S. Navy*

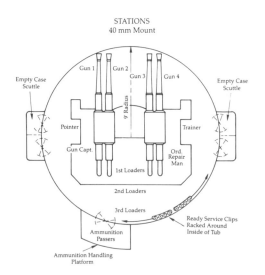

STATIONS
40 mm Mount

Empty Case Scuttle

Empty Case Scuttle

Gun 1   Gun 2   Gun 3   Gun 4

9' Radius

Pointer   Trainer

Gun Capt.   Ord. Repair Man

1st Loaders

2nd Loaders

3rd Loaders

Ready Service Clips Racked Around Inside of Tub

Ammunition Passers

Ammunition Handling Platform

Fig. 19. One of *Texas'* OS2U Kingfisher floatplanes approaches the ship to be recovered after a scouting mission over Iwo Jima, February 16, 1945. Another Kingfisher appears at the far right, atop No. 3 gun turret catapult. *Courtesy National Archives*

marked that "however firmly and stoutly you may build pill-boxes at the beach, they will be destroyed by bombardment of the main armament of the battleships. The power of American warships and aircraft makes every landing operation possible to whatever beachhead they like." *Texas* had its share in earning this reluctant tribute.

The battleship returned to Ulithi to prepare for the assault on Okinawa, in the Ryukyu Islands. Task Force 54 now included nine battleships and ten cruisers, with thirty-two destroyers and destroyer escorts. Aerial reconnaissance of Okinawa showed few beach defenses. The Japanese strategy on an island of any size was to fortify strong inland points, let the enemy land nearly unopposed, and then resist to the death in the strong points while waves of kamikazes (suicide planes) struck the supporting naval forces. The task force commander, Rear Adm. Morton Deyo, ordered his ships to use their observation planes to search out targets and to come as close as possible to the beaches for accurate shooting.

After midnight on March 26, 1945, the bombardment force moved into place off Okinawa. The first day's firing went well, though the big ships could not close the island before minesweepers cleared the inshore waters. For five days the ships hit their targets while carrier planes added punishing air strikes. Fire was slow and deliberate, the ships moving slowly or lying to and dropping shells on selected targets with the help of aerial spotters. During the nights the force withdrew from the beaches and took up antiaircraft formation offshore to wait for morning.

On the second day of the bombardment, kamikazes began to strike. One of them hit the battleship *Nevada* and put one of its turrets out of action, while other planes damaged a cruiser and two destroyers. It was the first day of a prolonged air-sea action in the battle for Okinawa.

By the fourth day of bombardment, the minesweepers had cleared the area to a point that ships could drop accurate fire at short range on airfields and other defenses. Frogmen blasted paths through beach obstacles under cover of gunfire. L-Day, as the landing day was called in this operation, was the first day of April. As the troops went ashore on Okinawa's west coast, *Texas* took part in a diversion off the southeastern side of the island to distract the defenders.

The landing was deceptively easy. The expected fierce resistance on the beaches did not materialize, and the advance inland ran far ahead of plan. The Japanese had concentrated their defenses in the northern and southern ends of the island, particularly in the southern portion around the towns of Naha and Shuri. The fighting on land ground down into a deadly yard-by-yard contest, while a kamikaze offensive from Japanese airfields, poetically named *kikusui* ("floating chrysanthemums") made life hellish for the support ships on which the troops depended for logistics and fire support. *Texas* was part of this action until May 14, 1945, fighting off suicide attacks at Okinawa on April 12 and near the small neighboring island of Ie Shima on April 16. As on Iwo Jima, the gunfire of *Texas* and its consorts had a powerful share in making the eventual victory possible.

Texas arrived in San Pedro Bay, Philippines, on May 17, 1945. There the ship made voyage repairs and prepared for the anticipated invasion of the Japanese home island of Kyushu,

Fig. 20. An OS2U Kingfisher is lifted from the water by *Texas'* starboard crane after the aircraft's return from a scouting mission over Iwo Jima on February 16, 1945. One of the aircraft's crewmen attaches lines used to guide the plane as it is moved back to the catapult on No. 3 gun turret. *Courtesy National Archives*

which was planned for October. In August, though, the United States dropped atomic bombs on the Japanese cities of Hiroshima and Nagasaki, and the Japanese surrendered. World War II was over. After a brief return to now-secured Okinawa, *Texas* sailed for Pearl Harbor to board veterans returning to the United States for discharge.

Navy Day, October 27, 1945, was a festive occasion at ports and naval bases throughout the country. *Texas* was on display

Fig. 21. In Leyte Gulf, Philippine Islands *Texas'* crew takes a well-deserved rest and gathers on the foredeck for a performance of the musical *Oklahoma* by a USO troupe, May 22, 1945. *Courtesy National Archives*

at San Pedro, California, and accommodated more than thirteen thousand visitors. Also in the immediate postwar months it made three transport runs to Pearl Harbor in what was called Operation Magic Carpet, carrying servicemen home. The ship's last transport voyage ended on Christmas Eve at San Diego. A month later it transited the Panama Canal to arrive at Norfolk in mid-February of 1946. At the Norfolk Naval Shipyard it was prepared for retirement—"mothballing."

Two years later *Texas* was towed to Texas' San Jacinto State

Park. On April 21, 1948—the anniversary of Texas independence—it was formally decommissioned and became a state memorial. Fleet Adm. Chester Nimitz, the principal speaker and a native Texan, noted that "it is particularly fitting that its final resting place be adjacent to these historic battlegrounds where so much of the Lone Star State's tradition was born."

For more than thirty years the ship had carried the name, and the honor, of the state of Texas from Veracruz to Okinawa, from the Denmark Strait to North Africa. *Texas'* final berth is, indeed, fitting.

Profiles

C. W. Nimitz
Fleet Admiral, USN

USS. TEXAS.
No. 18-62
3-18-3

Fig. 22. The first battleship *Texas* (commissioned in 1895) was short in relation to its beam. The forward 12-inch turret, seen here, is sponsored out over the ship's port side. The after turret was similarly "echeloned" out to starboard. Smaller guns were mounted on the deck and in hull casemates, and light guns for defense against torpedo boats were carried in the tops. *Courtesy U.S. Navy*

Fig. 23. Before World War I *Texas* showed a much trimmer profile than later in its career. This view, taken not long after its commissioning, shows an open bridge behind the armored conning tower as the highest point in the superstructure, searchlight platforms aligned vertically on the foremast, a few radio antennae wires strung to the cage masts, and 5-inch guns forward in the gun deck and at the stern. *Courtesy of the Mariners Museum, Newport News, Virginia*

Fig. 24. By December, 1916, when this photograph was taken at Hampton Roads, *Texas'* open bridge had received a cover; optical rangefinders were being tried atop turrets 2, 3, and 4; and the radio antennae were becoming more complex. The 3-inch antiaircraft guns at the tops of the crane kingposts, indicating the beginning of a shift toward a new kind of naval warfare, were the first on any U.S. battleship. Figures inked on the photograph indicate the height above the waterline of the 5-inch guns mounted on the gun deck amidships and astern. Service experience was to prove that those guns were difficult to use in any kind of sea, and all of them were eventually removed. *Courtesy U.S. Navy*

Fig. 25. After World War I *Texas* showed modifications based on its experience in the North Sea. Here the forward 5-inch guns have been removed and their ports sealed, and an enclosed navigation bridge as well as secondary-battery fire control stations have been added above the armored conning tower. Also note that the optical rangefinders have been reduced to two, located on the roof of the bridge and just aft of the mainmast. *Courtesy of The Mariners Museum, Newport News, Virginia*

Fig. 26. After *Texas* emerged from the shipyard in 1927, its appearance had changed considerably. This photograph was taken after the modernization but before the flag bridge and other pieces of superstructure were added above the navigation bridge on the foremast. *Courtesy U.S. Navy*

Fig. 27. Flags and pennants flying, *Texas* was at its pre–World War II best on October 27, 1940, after convoy duty in the Atlantic. The "bird baths" at the mast tops, which mounted four .50-caliber antiaircraft machine guns each, were installed about 1935, but the one on the foremast was removed again by 1942. *Courtesy National Archives*

Fig. 28. In 1943 *Texas* was assigned to escort the huge convoys of transport ships that were supplying the buildup of arms and men for the invasion of France and the assault on German-occupied Europe. Antiaircraft armament at that time included 1.1-inch "Chicago piano" quad mounts. The radar antennae atop the foremost and the after fire control top were for the FC main-battery ranging radar, but an optical rangefinder is still kept in reserve atop No. 4 turret. *Courtesy of The Mariners Museum, Newport News, Virginia*

Fig. 29. By the end of World War II, *Texas* was not a first-line battleship. However, studded with both bombardment and antiaircraft guns and with radar antennae, it was still a formidable support ship for the invasions that led to the defeat of Germany and Japan. As shown in this photograph, by 1945 it was painted in Camouflage Measure 21, the color it wears today. Included in the array of antennae are the SK-1 air search radar—the large "bedspring" antenna atop the mainmast—and the Mark 50 antiaircraft directors located on the masts. *Courtesy U.S. Navy*

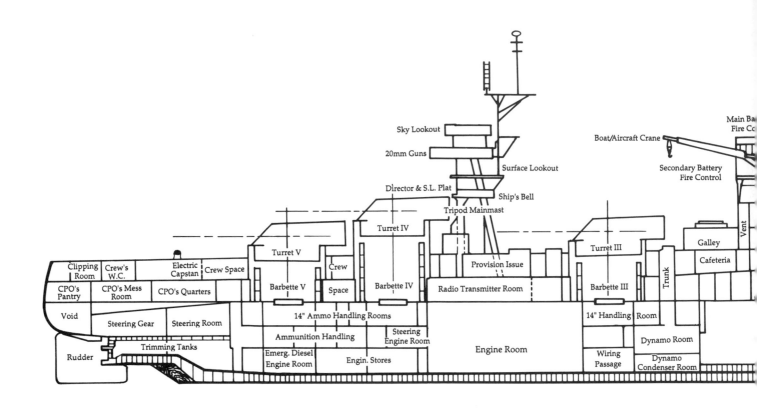

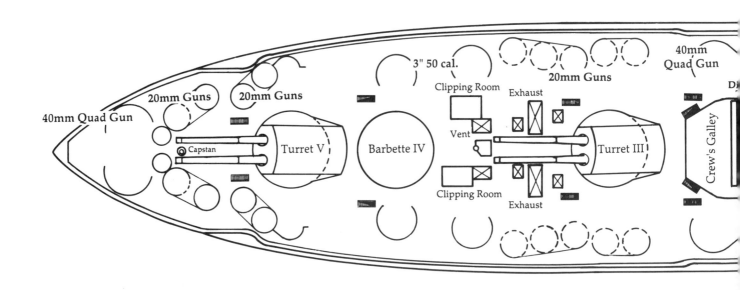

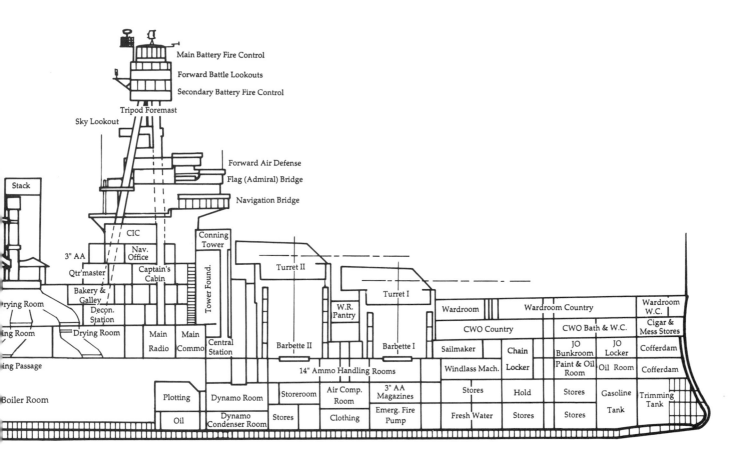

Main Battery Fire Control
Forward Battle Lookouts
Secondary Battery Fire Control
Tripod Foremast
Sky Lookout
Forward Air Defense
Flag (Admiral) Bridge
Navigation Bridge
Stack
CIC
Conning Tower
3" AA
Nav. Office
Turret II
Qtr'master
Captain's Cabin
Turret I
Wardroom
Wardroom Country
Wardroom W.C.
Bakery & Galley
Tower Found.
CWO Country
CWO Bath & W.C.
Cigar & Mess Stores
Decon. Station
W.R. Pantry
rying Room
Drying Room
Main Radio
Main Commo
Central Station
Barbette II
Barbette I
Sailmaker
Chain Locker
JO Bunkroom
JO Locker
Cofferdam
ing Room
ing Passage
14" Ammo Handling Rooms
Windlass Mach.
Paint & Oil Room
Oil Room
Cofferdam
Boiler Room
Plotting
Dynamo Room
Storeroom
Air Comp. Room
3" AA Magazines
Stores
Hold
Stores
Gasoline Tank
Trimming Tank
Oil
Dynamo Condenser Room
Stores
Clothing
Emerg. Fire Pump
Fresh Water
Stores
Stores

INBOARD PROFILE

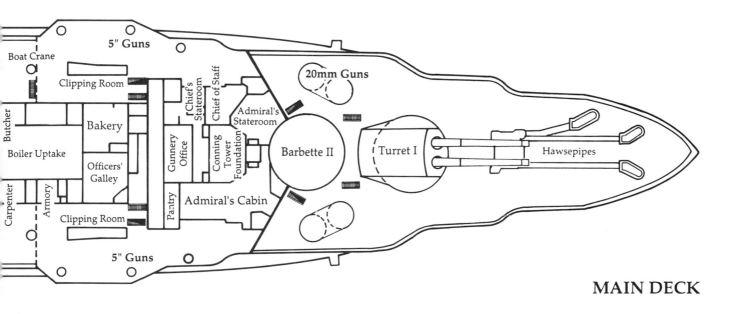

5" Guns
Boat Crane
Clipping Room
Chief's Stateroom
Chief of Staff
20mm Guns
Admiral's Stateroom
Butcher
Bakery
Gunnery Office
Conning Tower Foundation
Barbette II
Turret I
Hawsepipes
Boiler Uptake
Officers' Galley
Carpenter
Armory
Pantry
Admiral's Cabin
Clipping Room
5" Guns

MAIN DECK

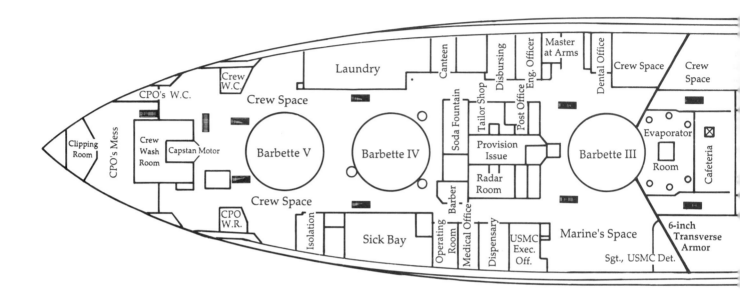

Crew
W.C.

Laundry

Canteen

Disbursing

Eng. Officer

Master
at Arms

Dental Office

Crew Space

Crew
Space

CPO's W.C.

Crew Space

Tailor Shop

Post Office

CPO's Mess

Clipping
Room

Crew
Wash
Room

Capstan Motor

Barbette V

Barbette IV

Soda Fountain

Provision
Issue

Barber

Barbette III

Evaporator
Room

Cafeteria

Crew Space

Radar
Room

CPO
W.R.

Isolation

Sick Bay

Operating
Room

Medical Office

Dispensary

USMC
Exec.
Off.

Marine's Space

6-inch
Transverse
Armor

Sgt., USMC Det.

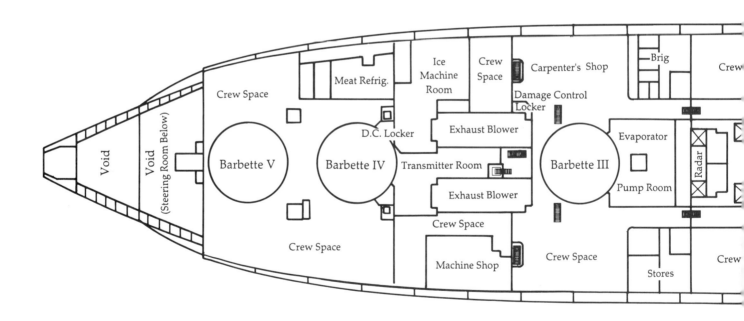

Crew Space

Meat Refrig.

Ice
Machine
Room

Crew
Space

Carpenter's Shop

Brig

Crew

Damage Control
Locker

Void

Void
(Steering Room Below)

Barbette V

Barbette IV

D.C. Locker

Exhaust Blower

Transmitter Room

Barbette III

Evaporator

Radar

Crew Space

Exhaust Blower

Pump Room

Crew Space

Crew Space

Machine Shop

Crew Space

Crew

Stores

Crew

50

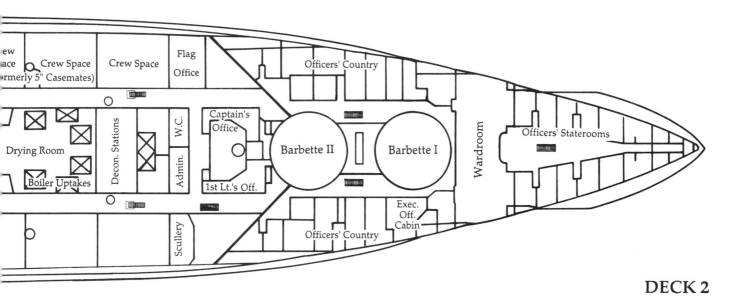

DECK 2

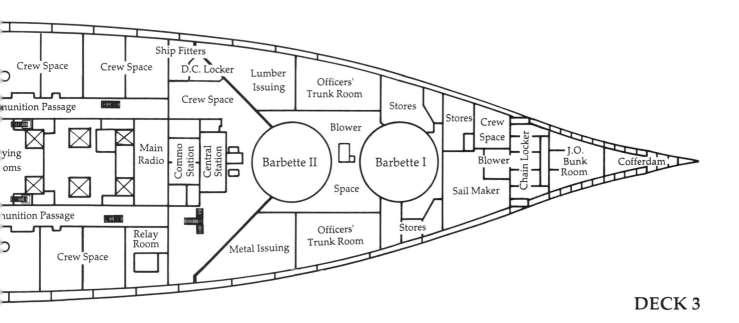

DECK 3

Plates

Plate 1. *Texas'* **Formal Portrait**

Go any day in early morning to the battleship *Texas*, stand on the bow, facing the superstructure, and the terrible power and grandeur of the dreadnought battleship becomes obvious. This weapon in military history was at once the most powerful of its time and yet was described in print with such terms as "handsome," "balanced," and even "graceful." *Texas* is the last of a kind, the sole surviving first-generation dreadnought in existence. (The first generation of dreadnoughts includes those ships built between 1906 and the commissioning of the first oil-burning ships in 1915.) It is the only intact ship in the world to have served in and survived both world wars. It is a National Historic Landmark and a National Historic Engineering Landmark as well, because its reciprocating steam engines are the last of their size to be found anywhere. And it was the first battleship given to its name state as a memorial. *Alabama, North Carolina,* and *Massachusetts* have followed the lead, but those ships, completed during or just before World War II, are not of the same vintage as *Texas.* And in that vintage lies the great benefit *Texas* can offer. It is an intact laboratory that mirrors the way we thought and fought in the tumultuous first half of this century.

Plate 2. General View, Starboard Side

The battleships *Texas* and *New York* composed the fifth class of American dreadnoughts built in the years prior to World War I. Authorized in 1910, *Texas'* keel was laid at Newport News (Va.) Shipbuilding and Drydock Company on April 17, 1911. The ship was launched May 18, 1912, and commissioned into service on March 12, 1914. *Texas* weighed twenty-seven thousand tons, was just over 565 feet long at the waterline, and was armed with ten 14-inch guns (this measure indicates the diameter of the gun's bore) and twenty-one 5-inch secondary guns. The main armored belt, a vertical sheet of carbon-hardened steel that protected the ship's vital areas, was ten to twelve inches thick. That combination of firepower and protection made *Texas* and *New York* the world's most powerful battleships. But in a world feverishly preparing for a great war at sea, their reign was brief. It lasted only until early 1915, when the British Royal Navy commissioned the first of its *Queen Elizabeth*–class ships, armed with 15-inch guns. This view of the ship shows the new mooring system installed following the restoration of 1988–90. The ship is locked into sliding collars that ride up and down on four posts as the tide rises and falls, ensuring that *Texas* will never again sink to the muddy bottom of its anchorage.

Plate 3. Foremast and Superstructure

Here, in the ship's forward tripod mast and superstructure, lay the brain of every dreadnought, the command and control system. The fire of its guns was directed from the "fighting top," the tri-level structure atop the mast. The ship's course and maneuvering were determined on the navigation bridge or in the armored conning tower. Entire fleets could be directed by their admirals from the flag bridge. When radar gained an integral role in the defense of American warships, the CIC (Combat Information Center) was located at the base of the tripod, just behind the armored conning tower. *Texas* did not begin service life with tripod masts. American dreadnoughts built prior to World War I displayed two cage masts of equal height. But these proved unsteady platforms for the fire control directors. After the battleship *Michigan*'s foremast collapsed in a North Atlantic gale in January, 1918, the cage design was dropped, and all American dreadnoughts converted to sturdier tripod masts. The forward superstructure contained the captain's quarters, inside on the level immediately below that of the conning tower. And *Texas* also provided admiral's quarters, now the Nimitz Room museum, on the main deck level right behind No. 2 turret.

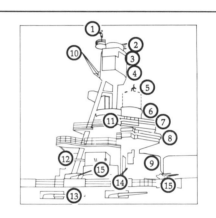

1. SG Surface Search Radar
2. Main Battery Fire Control
3. Forward Battle Lookouts
4. Secondary Battery Fire Control
5. Mark 50 Gunfire Director Radar Unit
6. Mark 50 Director Platfrom
7. Flag (Admiral's) Bridge
8. Navigation Bridge
9. Armored Conning Tower
10. Signal Flag Halyards
11. Mark 51 Optical Gun Director Tub
12. Combat Information Center (CIC)
13. 5-Inch/51 Calibre Secondary Guns
14. 3-Inch Antiaircraft Guns
15. 40mm Antiaircraft Quad Mount

Plate 4. Amidships Structures

Located immediately behind the forward tripod are the other structures that make up *Texas'* superstructure. The two ship's cranes handled the loading and unloading of supplies, the ship's small boats, and, after the 1925–27 refit, the ship's aircraft. In the last year of World War II, 20mm antiaircraft guns were mounted in the cupolas atop the cranes. *Texas* began life with two funnels. With the conversion to oil-fired boilers in 1925–27, though, all three boiler rooms were "trunked" into one funnel. This was done in part to facilitate the third structure shown here, the second of the ship's fire control and spotting stations. Originally located atop the mainmast, those functions were relocated during the 1925–27 refit, when the mainmast tripod wound up much shorter than the foremast. Prior experience had shown that funnel smoke obscured the mainmast fire control view, so this truss tower was constructed to contain those functions. The tower was similar in layout to the director station atop the foremast, except that the battle lookout level was omitted.

Plate 5. Mainmast or After Tripod

In naval terminology, "mainmast" refers to that structure located at the middle of the ship. *Texas'* second cage mast was located amidships, in front of No. 3 14-inch turret, and was designated the mainmast. But during the 1925–27 refit, it was found that the second tripod would not fit in that area, and so it was located between turrets 3 and 4. Space in which to mount the tripod legs was limited, and that restricted the height of the mast to just 44 feet above the deck, while the foremast reached 104 feet. In 1944–45, the upper platform of the mainmast mounted a Mark 50 gunfire control director, as did the platform above the flag bridge on the foremast. Both were removed from the ship prior to its donation to the state for a memorial in 1948. Other radar units include an SG surface search radar, at the very top of both the mainmast and the foremast, and an SK I "bedspring" radar for air search. Four searchlights were mounted on the lowest platform. During World War II, 20mm antiaircraft guns were mounted on the lookout (second) level of the mainmast. Both masts also carried concentration dials, resembling large clock faces, prior to the advent of radar.

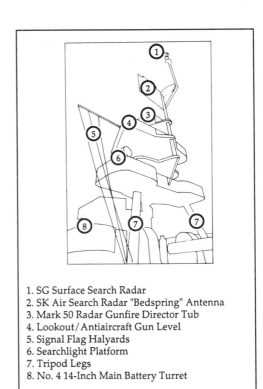

1. SG Surface Search Radar
2. SK Air Search Radar "Bedspring" Antenna
3. Mark 50 Radar Gunfire Director Tub
4. Lookout/Antiaircraft Gun Level
5. Signal Flag Halyards
6. Searchlight Platform
7. Tripod Legs
8. No. 4 14-Inch Main Battery Turret

Plate 6. Anchor Chains

Texas carried three anchors during its service career—two on the starboard side and one to port; all were connected to the capstan mechanism located in front of No. 1 turret on the ship's foredeck. Each anchor weighed 20,180 pounds and was attached to 840 feet of stud-link chain. Each anchor chain was composed of nine fifteen-fathom "shots" (a fathom is six feet). A five-fathom "swivel shot" was attached to the eye on the anchor's shank, or center column. Each link weighed 96 pounds. The wildcat brake on the capstans and pelican hooks, or quick release clamps, held the anchor in place until it was let go. The length of chain "paid out" when the ship was at anchor was at least twice the depth of the water, and it might be five to seven times the depth in heavy weather. The cable link shown above is one of several detachable links in each anchor cable. It could be separated for maintenance, to change the anchor configuration—for instance by dangling two anchors from the same cable—or to extend the length of any one cable beyond its normal 840 feet. When the ship was underway, the anchors were hauled in flush with the hull. The shank was inside the anchor hawse pipe, and only the flukes, or blades, were outside the hull. The cables were reeled into the chain locker, located in the bow of the ship.

Plate 7. Starboard Casemate Front

To leave *Texas'* foredeck and move aft, visitors must pass through one of the two upper casemate areas, located on each side of the superstructure. These casemates, not originally a part of *Texas'* design, were another modification undertaken during the 1925–27 refit. By that time, it had become apparent to all navies that the location of the secondary guns on any level below the upper deck made them unworkable in any but the smoothest waters. So six of *Texas'* 5-inch guns were moved from deck 2 to these enclosed casemates on the upper deck. Three guns were mounted on each side, and the second and third guns were sponsoned out over the ship's side to allow for wider arcs of fire. Armor protection within these casemates was limited to the thickness of a splinter shield. The casemate areas also provided ample foundations for *Texas'* growing antiaircraft battery. Shown here are the 3-inch high-angle antiaircraft guns, which are the single barrels above the 5-inch battery. Also shown, located above the ship's life ring, is one of the ten 40mm quad mounts with which *Texas* finished World War II.

Plate 8. 14-inch Gun Sleeve, General View

If the bridge of a dreadnought was its brain, the main gun battery was certainly its soul, its very reason for existence. All other aspects of design—speed, armor, accommodations—were subservient to the task of carrying that main battery into battle and keeping the guns firing until victory or destruction. The 14-inch/45-caliber guns mounted in *Texas* and *New York* represented a quantum leap in ordnance for the United States. The navy felt this change was necessitated by a similar British increase from 12- to 13.5-inch guns. This view shows the interior of the right-hand gunhouse sleeve in *Texas'* No. 3 turret. Shells arrived from the magazines nose down in the hoist at left. They were then tipped backward onto the tray apron, pointing into the gun breech. A hydraulic rammer (not shown) thrust the shell into the breech, followed by 420 pounds of cordite in four silk bags. Then the breech block, which alone weighed several tons, was closed and locked by hydraulic power. The guns usually were fired from the director control station atop the foremast, but in an emergency they could be fired in local control by the turret commander. The gunhouse was protected by fourteen inches of armor on the face plates, eight to nine inches on the sides, eight inches on the rear, and a four-inch roof.

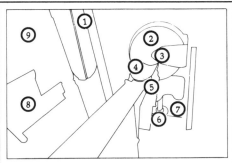

1. Shell Hoist
2. 14-inch/45 Calibre Gun Breech
3. Breech Locking Mechanism
4. Shell Tray
5. Spoon Tray (Collapsed)
6. Gun Elevating Screw
7. Working Chamber
8. Shell Tray Apron
9. Wall Separating Left and Right Sleeves of Gunhouse

Plate 9. 14-inch Shell and Cordite Charges

A 14-inch shell and the cordite propellant that unleashed it are shown on the loading trays in the left and right gun sleeves of *Texas'* No. 1 turret. In the left view, the spoon tray is folded. In battle it would be extended into the open gun breech to guide the shell and propellant and to protect the breech threads from damage by the 1,500-pound projectiles. The armor-piercing shell is capable of penetrating thirteen inches of protective steel. The donut-shaped pin in the rear of the shell is a removable padeye, used with chain hoists in the shell-handling room to transfer the shells from their nose-down storage position to the shell hoists. The four cordite bags in the right photo each weighed 105 pounds and arrived in a separate hoist that terminated below the working chamber. They were then passed upwards by hand through a scuttle into the gunhouse, where they were placed on the loading tray. The cordite was pushed into the breech with the padded end of a wooden pole to avoid accidental spark ignition. The right view also displays the intricacy of the breech block threads, an interrupted screw design that required only a partial turn to seal the breech. When fired, gases from the exploding cordite forced the shell out the gun muzzle at a velocity of twenty-six hundred feet per second, with startling accuracy at ranges up to twenty thousand yards from a maximum gun elevation of fifteen degrees.

Plate 10. Turret Working Chamber

While *Texas'* 14-inch/45-caliber guns (multiply the two to get the length of the gun's bore, 52.5 feet) were loaded from the upper gunhouse, hands-on control of their movement came from the working chamber immediately below the guns. This view was taken by photographer Jim Cruz in No. 5 turret. From here, two gun crew members, a pointer and a trainer, could train (rotate) the turret and elevate or depress the gun muzzles individually, in local control. When controlled by the directors atop the foremast, the turrets were moved by electrical signals sent from the director to a servomechanism. As the director moved to stay on the target, the guns automatically moved to the same bearing. Electric power trained the turret at a rate of a hundred degrees per minute and elevated the guns at four degrees per second. Maximum elevation was fifteen degrees and maximum depression was five degrees. A gun crew member worked from the saddle seat at left center, operating the clutch levers in front of him. The wire hopper on the left is the powder chute, used to deliver the cordite charges to the gun pit just above. The cylindrical object in the upper left quadrant of the picture is the bottom of the 14-inch gun. This section of each turret system is inside the barbette, which is a cylindrical tower of 12-inch armor plate that extended three levels deep into the ship.

Plate 11. Shell-handling Room, View 1

Three levels below *Texas*' upper deck are the magazine complexes, with a shell-handling room and four propellant chambers for each turret. This view shows, from left, the drum-like, flash-tight cordite baffle, which opened and closed to pass charges from the magazines into the handling room; the magazine door; shell storage rooms; the base of the turret assembly and lower shell hoists; and the hoist control signal at upper right. The curved track in the ceiling is the pathway along which shells traveled from the storage rooms to the base of the hoist system. At the next level above this room, the shells were transferred to an inclined "pusher hoist" that lifted them to the gunhouse behind the center of rotation for the turret. During combat operations in World War II, *Texas*' main battery fired 4,278 rounds in support of amphibious and ground operations. Nearly half that total, 2,019 rounds, was expended during six weeks of operations off Okinawa. *Texas* also fired 923 rounds at the island of Iwo Jima and 892 rounds on D-Day and in subsequent operations off the coast of Normandy. The ship fired 273 rounds in support of the North African landings and 172 rounds along the coast of southern France.

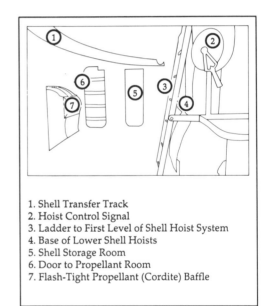

1. Shell Transfer Track
2. Hoist Control Signal
3. Ladder to First Level of Shell Hoist System
4. Base of Lower Shell Hoists
5. Shell Storage Room
6. Door to Propellant Room
7. Flash-Tight Propellant (Cordite) Baffle

72

Plate 12. Shell-handling Room, View 2

Shells for *Texas'* main battery were stored nose down in rooms under each turret, shown above on the left. The magazine complex for No. 5 turret has spaces for 116 shells in each of two storage rooms, and for another 30 on the shell deck of the hoist system. Those figures would be typical for the "low" turrets, 1, 3, and 5. The "high" turrets, 2 and 4, probably accommodated more, since their greater height above the main deck provided another storage level in the hoists. To fire those shells, *Texas* probably carried, at any one time, more than half a million pounds of high explosive propellant. Little wonder a single lucky hit in this area could obliterate a dreadnought. This happened to the British battlecruiser *Hood* in an engagement in May of 1941 with Germany's *Bismarck* in the Denmark Straits. To protect against such disasters—just three men survived the *Hood*—designers built in safeguards, like the tub in the right foreground. In an engagement, the tub was filled with water, and broken cordite bags or loose powder were dumped into it. More important were the baffles built into each level of the hoist system. These baffles closed automatically behind the shells and charges as they rose to the gunhouse. This prevented cordite flashes, from a hit on a turret, from traveling down the hoist system to the magazines.

Plate 13. Propellant Baffle Control

Two points of interest aboard *Texas* are detailed in this photograph from No. 2 shell-handling room. The marked knob controls the propellant baffles, the drum-like structures built into the walls of the shell-handling rooms and shown in plates 11 and 12. Designed to be flash-tight, the baffles are hollow. They opened or closed on both sides of the wall separating the shell room and propellant magazines. Reading the dial counterclockwise, "Send Powder" told the magazine crew to load the 105-pound cordite charges into the baffle. "Return Powder" sent the charge back into the magazine. "Stand By" told the magazine crew to prepare to send powder, and "Secure" meant to re-store all charges. The charges were contained in silk bags because that material burned most evenly. Crewmen in flash-protective suits moved charges manually from the baffle to the separate propellant hoist. To the right of the baffle control is a metal plate marked "FR 41." This designates the position of one of the ship's "ribs," the U-frames rising from the keel that support the ship's weight, like the frame of a house. Frames were numbered sequentially from the bow. A total of 140 frames supports *Texas'* weight—more than thirty thousand tons.

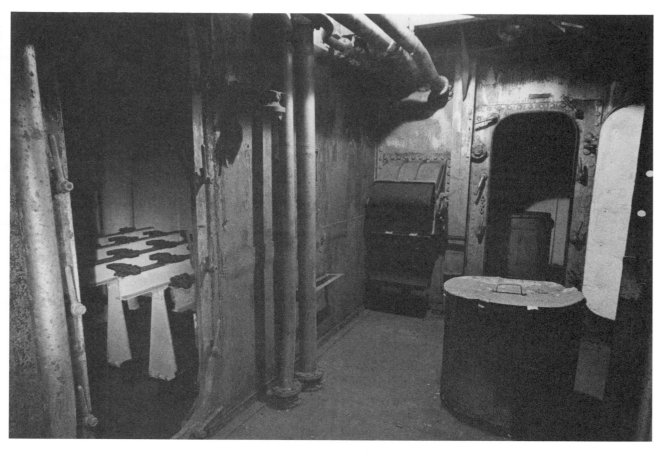

Plate 14. Armored Casemate Door

The great advance it presented in protective armor was a major reason the appearance of HMS *Dreadnought* in 1906 so revolutionized naval thinking. Yet no aspect of *Texas* is less visible than the armor. Like the lining of a well-made jacket, dreadnought armor is "sewn" into the shell of the ship, making it virtually invisible. The best available examples on *Texas* are the transverse bulkheads and armored doors that enclose the upper casemate area on deck 2. Constructed of carbon-hardened steel, the doors are always closed on that side of the ship engaging the enemy. On deck 2 the casemate extends from just behind No. 2 barbette to just forward of No. 3 barbette and varies from six and a half to nine inches in thickness. A similar armored "box," nine to eleven inches thick, encloses a lengthier portion of deck 3. Separate from these casemates is the main armored belt, a vertical sheet of steel, its face hardened by carbonizing, twelve inches thick at the top and ten inches thick at the bottom. It extends almost the full length of the hull from two feet above the waterline to nearly six feet below it. This was the ship's primary protection for the vital machinery spaces and the ammunition magazines. The total weight of *Texas'* armor exceeded seven thousand tons, or nearly a quarter of the ship's designed weight.

Plate 15. 5-inch Gun Positions

On *Texas'* starboard side, the present position of the remaining 5-inch secondary guns is contrasted with their former location, the circular, plated-over casemate area at left, on the second deck. Most dreadnoughts built prior to World War I carried their secondary battery on the second deck, or gun deck, and *Texas* and *New York* were no exceptions. Since the mounting position was universal among the great powers, all navies learned the same lesson at the same time: the secondary guns were too close to the water, the casemates flooded, and the guns could not be worked in any but the smoothest seas. Between the world wars, modernization of the ships addressed this problem, usually by moving the guns to a higher level. This modification was performed on *Texas* during the 1925–27 refit. At that time its secondary battery had been reduced from twenty-one to sixteen guns, and six of these were raised to the upper deck, where the main deckhouse was widened to provide a common enclosure. By August of 1942 only those six guns remained in *Texas'* secondary battery. Notice also the antiaircraft gun director tub on the main deck, reinstalled during the recent restoration work.

Plate 16. 5-inch Secondary Guns

Perhaps no aspect of dreadnought design was more debated than the secondary battery. This view shows the starboard (right side) casemate area of *Texas*, mounting three of the six 5-inch guns with which the ship finished its career. But dreadnoughts in their purest form were never intended to have a secondary battery. Early dreadnought advocates wanted ships that carried just one caliber of gun—the largest available. At the same time, there was the realization that dreadnoughts could be crippled by smaller, cheaper weapons, like the six-hundred-ton torpedo boats that evolved into today's modern destroyers. A dreadnought's guns could not be depressed low enough—or fired fast enough—to stop mass attacks by such boats. So the secondary battery was present even in 1906 on HMS *Dreadnought*, which gave its name to the whole lineage of ships that followed. When commissioned, *Texas* mounted a secondary battery of twenty-one 5-inch guns, nineteen located on the second deck. Two guns were mounted on each side of the forward wardroom; five were on each side behind the six-inch armor of the upper casemate; two were on each side aft of No. 5 14-inch barbette; and one was in an unprotected centerline casemate firing directly astern. The remaining two were mounted on the first superstructure deck, one on each side, between No. 2 14-inch turret and the bridge.

Plate 17. Gun Crew Artifact

If visitors are alert, reminders of the teeming life that filled *Texas* for thirty-four years can be found throughout the ship, often in unexpected places. Here, the names of the gun crew remain stamped into the steel support column of the gunner's chest pad on No. 2 5-inch gun in the port (left) casemate area. Warship gun crews, especially those on the smaller weapons, became close-knit groups for the most obvious of reasons: their very survival depended on the ability of each man to do his job well. A 5-inch gun crew included eleven men, and the work was labor-intensive. Unlike the giant 14-inch turrets, where the guns were operated by electric power and hydraulics, the secondary guns were operated manually. The fifty-pound projectiles were passed down a chain of human hands from the shell hoists to the gun breech, and that chain employed most of the gun's crew. Good crews could fire eight to ten rounds per minute, a rate required to stop the mass attacks of torpedo boats and destroyers, which were steadily increasing in size. As the inscribed names in this picture suggest, a well-drilled, successful gun crew was one in which each man took pride in his work.

Plate 18. 5-inch Shell Hoist

This view shows one of the 5-inch shell hoists that served the guns of *Texas'* secondary battery. A separate hoist served each gun in order to obtain the high rate of fire needed to stop small, high-speed craft attacking with torpedoes. The hoist shown above does not serve the 5-inch gun in the background, but No. 2 gun, out of view of the right of the picture. The shell boxes are lightly armored with splinter shields. When the guns were not in action, the hoists were completely closed by the double face cover shown here. At a maximum elevation of twenty degrees, the 5-inch/51-caliber guns could fire their fifty-pound shells to ranges of 12,000 to 17,100 yards (seven to ten miles), depending on the type of shell used. Both high-capacity and common shells were used, and the explosive charge of the high capacity was 13.2 pounds, or more than a quarter of the shell's weight. The propellant charge weighed 24.5 pounds and produced a muzzle velocity of 3,150 feet per second. *Texas'* secondary battery fired 3,885 rounds during combat operations in World War II. This was an impressive total, considering that only six 5-inch guns remained on the ship by August, 1942. Okinawa was the target for 2,640 rounds, 976 rounds were fired at Iwo Jima, and 272 rounds were fired during the Normandy invasion.

Plate 19. 3-inch Antiaircraft Guns

The first generation of dreadnought battleships was built with no consideration for the dangers later posed by the airplane, so no antiaircraft guns were included in the first-generation designs. Yet as early as 1917, some attention was given to the air threat. In that year *Texas* acquired its first antiaircraft guns, eight 3-inch Mark 21 models for use against the zeppelins used as scouts by the German navy. That battery increased to ten guns in December, 1941, and remained at that level for the rest of the ship's service life. The gun was a dual-purpose — meaning it could also be used against surface targets — pedestal type in an open mount with manual training and elevation. Maximum elevation was eighty-five degrees, and maximum depression was minus thirteen degrees. The guns fired 13.1-pound shells, in armor-piercing, high capacity, and antiaircraft variations, with a surface range of seven miles and an antiaircraft ceiling of 29,800 feet at eighty-five degrees elevation. The propellant charges weighed four pounds, muzzle velocity was 2,700 feet per second, and the rate of fire was twelve to fifteen rounds per minute. In their antiaircraft role, the guns proved relatively ineffective against the high-speed aircraft *Texas* encountered in World War II.

Plate 20. 40mm Antiaircraft Gun Mount

The rapid advances in the speed and power of aircraft, as well as their stunning early successes against surface ships in World War II, led to rapid increases in the antiaircraft batteries of all warships, including dreadnoughts. *Texas* added quad 1.1-inch antiaircraft gun mounts as early as January, 1941, but these "Chicago pianos" tended to jam as they heated up at higher rates of fire. The 1.1's were gradually replaced by the 40mm quad mount, a gun originally designed by the Swedish firm of Bofors and manufactured under license in the United States. *Texas* substituted ten 40mm quad mounts for its eight 1.1's in July, 1943. The 40mm mounts were capable of either power or manual operation, and fire control was either manual or by local directors (see plate 15). The guns fired a 4.8-pound shell with a muzzle velocity of 2,890 feet per second to a surface range of more than five miles and an antiaircraft ceiling of 22,800 feet at ninety degrees elevation. Rate of fire was 160 rounds per minute. The 40mm mounts proved so successful that all Allied navies had adopted them in some numbers by the end of World War II.

Plate 21. 20mm Antiaircraft Guns

Soon after the outbreak of World War II, warship designers recognized the need for close air defense. Since surface vessels most often came under attack from dive and torpedo bombers, rather than high-altitude level bombers, very high rates of fire were needed to fend off these fast, agile attackers. *Texas'* first "machine gun battery" had eight .50-caliber weapons mounted in January, 1941. Like the 1.1-inch quad mounts, these proved unreliable and ineffective, lacking the punch to penetrate the increasing armor of modern warplanes. In December, 1941, the .50's were replaced with the more powerful 20mm mounts. Often referred to as "heavy machine guns," they were actually light cannon with a high rate of fire. The gun was designed by another Swedish firm, Oerlikon, and built under license in the United States. The projectiles weighed more than a quarter of a pound, and they achieved a muzzle velocity of 2,740 feet per second and a fire rate of 450 rounds per minute. The surface range exceeded two miles, and the antiaircraft ceiling was ten thousand feet at ninety degrees elevation. These weapons, perhaps more than any other, kept Japan's kamikaze suicide planes from achieving wider success, since at close range and in massed batteries, the 20mm could literally shoot a plane to pieces before it could crash into its target.

Plate 22. Navigation Bridge

The navigation bridge was where the captains of *Texas* spent most of their time in general, and all of their time in battle. Here also was where the ship incurred its only battle casualty in two world wars, twenty-one-year-old helmsman Christian N. Christiansen. He died when an 11-inch shell from a German shore battery struck the armored conning tower, exploded upward, wrecked the bridge, and wounded thirteen others while *Texas* was providing fire support for American troops advancing on the port of Cherbourg, France. Subtle evidence of the damage can still be seen. *Texas'* bridge windows were square before that engagement on June 25, 1944. Round windows were installed when the bridge was repaired, but the outlines of the square windows still can be seen. *Texas* began its service career with a much smaller bridge, open except for a roof, fitted to the front side of the forward cage mast. Even before the end of World War I, this proved inadequate. It was replaced by a larger, enclosed pilothouse and chart room, with windows and small open wing areas on each side. The open catwalk around the outside of the bridge was added during the 1925–27 refit, and the flag bridge above the navigation bridge was added shortly thereafter.

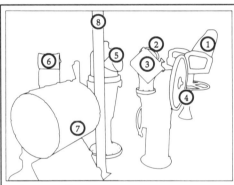

1. Captain's Chair
2. Gyrocompass
3. Rudder Angle Indicator
4. Helm Wheel
5. Compass Binnacle
6. Starboard Engine Telegraph
7. Port Engine Telegraph
8. Support Stanchion

Plate 23. Armored Conning Tower

Throughout the dreadnought era, great attention was paid to the protection of the command-and-control staff of battleships. The solution seemed to lie in the heavily armored command station, called the armored conning tower, to which the captain and his staff could relocate in battle. But few dreadnought commanders used them. The already limited view through the three-inch-wide slits was further obscured by shell splashes and cordite smoke. Most captains preferred the wider vistas of their unarmored bridges, and conning tower space was always restricted. The front half accommodated navigation, while the area behind the wall at left was devoted to fire control. The hatch visible near the helm wheel led down an armored trunk to central station, an armored secondary facility for command and control of the ship, located on deck 3. *Texas* and *New York* were the first U.S. dreadnoughts to adopt this protected "plot," largely because the range at which ships could engage each other was increasing as the size of the guns increased. Ironically, the thin splinter armor surrounding central station would have been vulnerable to plunging shellfire, the inevitable consequence of increasing gunnery ranges.

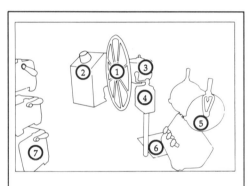

1. Hydraulic Helm Wheel
2. Radar Unit
3. Compass Binnacle
4. Electrical Steering Control
5. Engine Telegraph
6. Hatch to Central Station Trunk
7. Wall Separating Navigation and Fire Control Functions

Plate 24. Conning Tower Fire Control

This instrument panel located in the armored conning tower was one of many used to keep track of the fire of *Texas'* main battery guns. Each circular dial displayed the bearing on which that gun turret was firing at any given time. Another instrument in the tower's fire control section displayed the target range, and a light panel showed when each gun was ready to fire. Ideally, director firing controlled *Texas'* fifteen-thousand-pound full broadsides. Located at the top of the foremast and in the secondary tower abaft of the funnel, the directors consisted of both mechanical and optical instruments that took constantly adjusted bearings and ranges on the target. That information was fed to the main gun plot, located below the armored deck 3, and onto the plotting table, a mechanical computer that calculated the course and speed of both its own ship and the target, then projected where the target should be at the end of the flight time of the 14-inch shells. The plot also considered such variables as the heat of the guns—which altered ballistic properties after prolonged firing—local magnetic variations, barometric pressure, and even the rotation of the earth. Elevation of the guns and the lead, or bearing on which they would fire, could be calculated in seconds and fed to the gun turrets.

Plate 25. Radar Room

If any single advance in warfare technology could be credited with the Allied victory in World War II, it would be radar. *Texas* was in the forefront of naval radar development, as one of the first U.S. ships —and the first battleship—to carry radar. The radar room on the starboard side of deck 2, aft of No. 3 barbette, displays just some of the radar systems used by *Texas*. From left are the plot table, where air and surface radar contacts were tracked; the SK I air search radar set; and two units of the SG surface search radar. *Texas'* first radar was an experimental air search unit developed by Radio Corporation of America, designated CZX, and installed in January of 1939. SC radar replaced it early in 1942. This was in turn replaced in 1943 by the SK I, which used the "bedspring" antenna atop the after tripod mast. Two SG surface search sets were installed early in 1942, with antennas at the tip of both masts. Two Mark 3 fire control units were added in 1942 to direct *Texas'* 14-inch guns, with antennas atop both director control towers. Mark 50 fire control directors, for the 3-inch antiaircraft guns and as backup for the main battery, were installed in platforms on both masts before *Texas* was transferred to the Pacific in November, 1944.

Plate 26. Radar Set Detail

The SK I air search radar shown above was the busiest unit on *Texas* after the ship joined the Pacific fleet in late 1944. During this time Japan, desperate to slow the tide of U.S. victories, unleashed its airmen in kamikaze (literally, "divine wind") suicide attacks on U.S. warships. The SK radar had a range of roughly seventy-five miles and included an IFF, International Friend or Foe, recognition system. Air contacts showed up on the screen at lower left. The range of the contact was monitored on the screen and dials at upper left and the bearing on the dial at upper right. Notification of a contact went immediately to the ship's Combat Information Center (CIC), where the target also appeared on a "repeater" scope like the one in the lower left here. CIC then transferred the information onto its gun plot, a duplicate of the plot table shown in plate 25. From there, the information went to the Mark 50 directors, which provided more accurate control of the heavy 3-inch/50 caliber antiaircraft guns. The fire of the 40mm and 20mm antiaircraft batteries was not directed by radar. Each 40mm mount was controlled by an optical Mark 51 gun director tub, while the 20mm guns were under the local control of their crews.

Plate 27. Main Radio Room

Second only to advances in radar were advances in communications in World War II. Ship-to-ship communication and contact with distant bases were especially vital in the vast stretches of the Pacific Ocean. On board *Texas,* communications were centered on deck 3, well within the ship's "armored citadel." This view shows the main radio room, in operation twenty-four hours a day monitoring and reporting traffic on a wide range of frequencies. Research is continuing into the radio equipment used during *Texas'* career, but a preliminary listing compiled by the historic sites division of the Texas Parks and Wildlife Department produced a typewritten list more than a quarter of an inch thick. During World War I, most ship-to-ship communication was by signal flags from the ship's halyard lines. But it is likely *Texas* also had radio during that period. During World War II, it could use those same halyards, as well as signal lamps and probably a TBS (talk between ships) telephone system. *Texas* was the first vessel to broadcast a Voice of Freedom message, which is another unique distinction. On November 8, 1942, the ship transmitted a plea from Gen. Dwight D. Eisenhower urging Vichy French troops not to resist Operation Torch, the landings by United States forces in North Africa.

Plate 28. After Steering Compartment

If battle damage prevented a dreadnought commander from conning (controlling the movements) his ship from the forward control positions, he could, in theory, retreat to this emergency steering compartment. It is located on a platform level just below deck 3 in the stern of the ship. Here, from left to right, are the compass binnacle located on the emergency steering platform; the electric power switch panel and motors that engaged the twin screw-rams that operated the rudder; and the four-tiered wheel used to steer the ship if both the electric and hydraulic systems failed. These linked wheels, nearly six feet high, required sixteen men to operate, but slowly and tortuously the ship could be maneuvered in a limited way using pure muscle power. Realistically, if such efforts were needed, the survival of the ship already was in doubt. The door at the far end leads to the rudder post compartment, where *Texas'* rudder gauge permanently reads fifteen degrees to starboard. That was the rudder's angle when the ship came to rest in its San Jacinto berth in 1948, and time and the elements have frozen it in that position forever.

Plate 29. Captain's Cabin

The captain's cabin is located on the 02 level in the superstructure. It was the center for staff meetings and senior officer activity and decision making on *Texas*. The doorway at left leads to the captain's pantry. The corridor leads to an office area, and the door at right opens onto stairways that lead to the navigation bridge and armored conning tower. The captain's sleeping quarters, or stateroom, were located on the port side on the 01 level of the superstructure. Another small cubicle with a bunk was located on the starboard side, aft of the navigation bridge, where the captain could rest without leaving the command area. *Texas* had twenty-eight different commanding officers during the thirty-two years of its active service career. The first five commanders, Albert W. Grant, John Hood, Victor Blue, Nathan C. Twining, and Frank H. Schofield, all had destroyers named after them. Blue commanded *Texas* during its active service in World War I. During World War II, the ship had six commanders. Capt. Charles A. Baker was in command of the ship during its most active period of the war, from March, 1944, to August, 1945. Captain Baker also returned to command the ship on April 21, 1948, the day it was decommissioned and transferred to the state of Texas.

Plate 30. Officers' Country

Texas' executive officer occupied this cabin, located on the starboard side of deck 2, outboard of No. 1 barbette. Though somewhat larger, it was typical of the senior officers' cabins located in "officers' country" on both sides of deck 2, just aft of the wardroom. Junior officers were berthed on the starboard side of the half-deck forward of the wardroom, with warrant officers occupying the port side of the same area. Officers aboard a battleship were divided into four groups, not including flag officers (admirals) and their staff personnel. Commissioned officers were graduates of the Naval Academy at Annapolis and commanded operational areas of the ship, like engineering and gunnery. Staff officers were college graduates in the practice of their professions, such as medical and dental officers and chaplains. Warrant officers were former enlisted men who had distinguished themselves in specialty areas, such as carpentry, electronics, pharmacy, and gunnery, and had been placed in command of a division. Chief petty officers (CPOs) were the navy's non-commissioned officers, much like sergeants in the army, and also had experience in specialty areas.

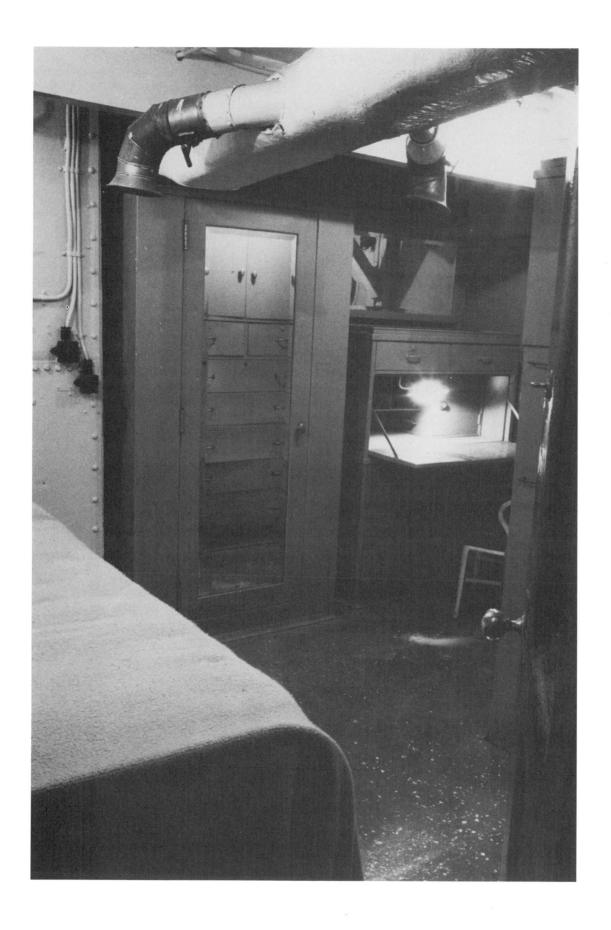

Plate 31. Forward Wardroom

During its service career, *Texas'* forward wardroom served as the senior officers' mess. Today it contains artifacts of the ship's history. The cabinet at left encases a silver service presented by the schoolchildren of Texas at Galveston on November 6, 1914, and an identical service presented by the citizens of Waco the same year. Except for two pieces, all the silver carries the star of Texas. The ship's bell at right is from the first battleship *Texas.* Built between 1889 and 1895 at Norfolk, it was the first true battleship built by the United States. In a wall niche is a 1/100-scale silver model of *DeSeven Provincien,* flagship of Dutch naval hero Adm. Michiel de Ruyter from 1666 to 1674. It was a gift from the Holland America Line after *Texas* rescued the passengers and crew of the foundering steamer *Ryndam* off Nantucket on May 26, 1915. A painting of the ship's mascot, a boxer named "Jim," adorns a wall on the port side. Painted by Maud Earl "as a tribute from an Englishwoman to the American Navy," it was presented to *Texas* by Adm. David Beatty, commander of the British Grand Fleet, while *Texas* served with that force in World War I.

Plate 32. Crew Space

Personal space for enlisted men was always at a premium on warships, and with an expanded crew of just over eighteen hundred by the end of World War II, *Texas* was no different. These pipe frame bunks, or "spring racks," hung in virtually every open area on and above deck 3. Hammocks were the bedding for U.S. Navy seamen when *Texas* joined the fleet. By 1939 the Navy Bureau of Medicine and Surgery had concluded that hammocks caused back problems, and it prescribed spring racks. But in the more crowded conditions of World War II, the hammock remained in use. Racks were assigned on a seniority basis, and those without racks used hammocks and cots. Hammocks were stored during the day and reissued in the evening. Enlisted berthing areas, like most of the ship other than officers' country, were painted white. The decks were red, following a traditional belief that crewmen would not be as shocked by the sight of blood if it were not obvious against a different deck color. Enlisted men were berthed as near their assigned stations as possible, and the old 5-inch gun casemates on deck 2 and coal bunkers on deck 3 were converted to crew space after the 1925–27 refit. Each enlisted man was assigned a locker to stow his personal gear.

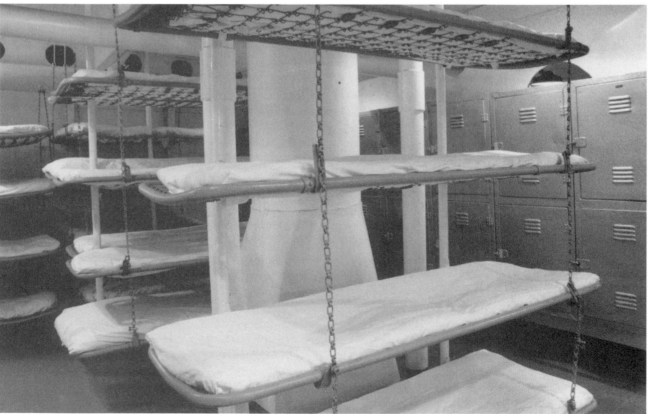

Plate 33. Knot Tying

This Turk's head knot tied around a stanchion on the starboard side of deck 2 is one of the few purely decorative items to be found aboard *Texas*. The knots are wrapped around the tops of brass tubes that are used to decorate part of the stanchion. The Turk's head covers the lip of the tube and prevents it from slipping to the deck. Both the brass and knots were referred to as "fancy work," and battleships tended to have more fancy work than other types of warships. Knots themselves are among the oldest forms of fancy work on naval vessels. Most of the knots on any ship were tied by the bosun's mates. Depending on the mate's skills, they could take from thirty to forty-five minutes to tie. Paint was applied to prevent the knots from absorbing grime into the fiber of the "small line" used to tie them. Many of the knots on *Texas* have been restored by Nate Cloutman, a battleship *Texas* volunteer and former Parks and Wildlife Department employee who served aboard cruisers during World War II. A large display of nautical knots is located in a glass case on the starboard side of deck 2, aft of No. 2 barbette.

Plate 34. Main Galley

Perhaps no aspect of life on board a warship was more important to its crew than the quality and quantity of food. Like all dreadnoughts, *Texas* was designed with special attention to that issue. And as the size of the crew expanded from just over a thousand men in 1914 to more than eighteen hundred by the end of World War II, *Texas'* food service evolved to provide for them. The main galley was located on the upper deck, a common site in dreadnoughts. Fire was a constant concern, so the most obvious source of fire always was located on the highest deck possible. The main galley prepared food in four double-oven navy standard lightweight ranges, on the right. These were oil-burning units manufactured by B. B. Buell & Co. of Seattle, Washington, and installed aboard *Texas* in 1944. Soups, boiled vegetables, and starches were prepared in eight large cauldrons, one of which is shown on the left. Located adjacent to the galley on the ship's port side were a butcher shop and bakery. A 1935 ship's roster listed twenty-six commissary personnel, including cooks, specialty cooks, bakers, and butchers. There were also thirty-eight mess stewards, who, among their duties, delivered the food to the officers' mess areas.

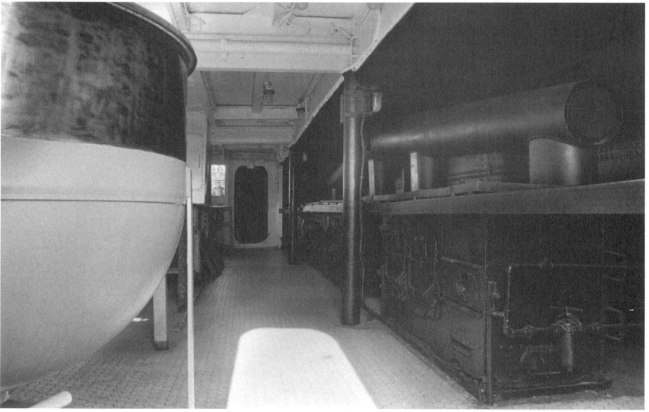

Plate 35. Cafeteria

With more than eighteen hundred men to feed by 1944, *Texas'* food distribution system required expansion. A new cafeteria was installed on deck 2, directly beneath the main galley, during the ship's refit in New York in the fall of 1944. Food was transferred from the galley to the cafeteria by a dumbwaiter, seen at left rear, and kept warm in steam tables. Crewmen were served on metal trays, which they took to their berthing areas. Divisional mess cooks also collected food from the cafeteria. Each enlisted berthing area included six mess tables, each seating ten men, with one mess cook for every two tables. Mess cooks received five dollars a month additional pay; a good mess cook—one who made sure his mess mates got seconds—could earn as much as twenty dollars a month in tips. Before the cafeteria, food was collected directly from the main galley. Commissioned officers, warrant officers, and chief petty officers (CPOs) ate in separate mess areas, where food was delivered by mess stewards. Food for the ranking officers was prepared in a separate galley, located inside the starboard "Air Castle" on the main deck. Senior officers, lieutenants and above, ate in the main wardroom on deck 2. The junior officers' mess was located forward of the wardroom on the starboard side, and the warrant officers' mess was to port. Commissioned and warrant officers paid for their meals, while the navy paid for feeding the rest of the crew.

Plate 36. Soda Fountain and Canteen

The quality of navy food varied from ship to ship, but in general it was better on larger warships, which also had space available for canteens and soda fountains. The one on *Texas* was on the port side of deck 2 just forward of No. 4 barbette. Restoration is continuing in this area, known to *Texas'* crewmen as the "Geedunk Stand." The soda fountain included a malted milk mixer, Coca-Cola dispenser, and freezers equipped with early refrigeration units. In addition to soft drinks, the fountain served ice cream in a variety of concoctions, including the classic "Dixie Cups" and ice cream sodas made from milk or milk substitutes. The price was ten cents a portion. The canteen, located on the port side opposite the soda fountain, provided candy, called "pogie bait," shaving supplies, and tobacco. Cigarettes were a nickel a pack or fifty cents a carton, and candy bars cost five cents. Purchases could be made in cash or with chits—tokens purchased through the ship's services operation that could be used in several service areas. The chits were turned in for reimbursement at regular intervals by the operators of service facilities, such as the soda fountain or tailor shop. The ship's services operation was under the direction of the supply officer, usually a junior commissioned officer.

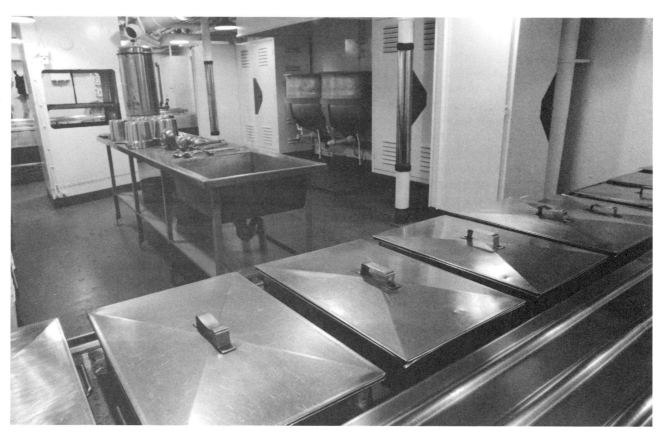

Plate 37. Operating Room

The operating room shown in this photograph by Jim Cruz was only one part of a complete facility for medical diagnosis and treatment aboard *Texas*. Adjacent to the operating room on the starboard side of deck 2, aft of No. 3 barbette, were the twenty-bed sick bay, an isolation ward with fourteen beds, a dispensary for distributing medication, and suitable areas for medical records, examinations, and immunizations. Dental facilities were located on the port side of deck 2, outboard of No. 3 barbette. The ship's medical staff was headed by a physician with surgical training and the rank of commander or lieutenant commander. He was assisted by perhaps one more physician, hospital corpsmen, and pharmacist's mates. The most common ailments were shipboard injuries and venereal disease. All medical care was free, and battleships also were expected to provide services for Marine landing parties, crews from smaller vessels like destroyers, and prisoners of war. In ship-to-ship combat, battle casualties would be brought first to auxiliary dressing stations. On *Texas* these were located on deck 3, in the starboard crew space outboard of central station, and in starboard compartment D109, outboard on No. 4 barbette.

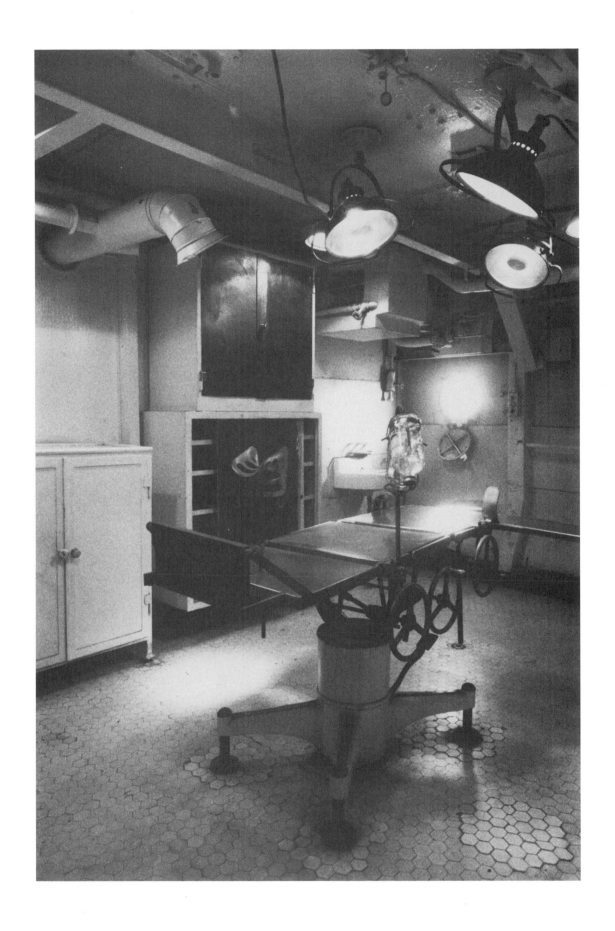

Plate 38. Barber Shop

Texas' barber shop, located on the starboard side of deck 2 just forward of No. 4 barbette, has been restored with the recent addition of two period barber chairs. The barber shop originally was located just aft of the dentist's office on the starboard side of deck 2, and it had four chairs. Only larger warships had barber shops, but the navy's concerns with hair length were specific enough to merit this entry in the 1943 *Bluejacket's Manual:* "The hair, beard and mustache must be worn neatly trimmed. The face must be kept clean shaved, except a mustache or beard and mustache may be worn at discretion. No eccentricities in the manner of wearing the hair, beard or mustache are allowed." And none were. Crewmen paid a twenty-five-cent chit for a regulation crew cut or shave, often done by shipmates who had not been barbers in civilian life. Regulation length was a requirement for "liberty," going ashore when the ship was in port. But some men gambled that they could avoid the watchful eye of officers and senior petty officers, and they paid shipmates cash for slightly longer cuts, which were given in working and berthing compartments throughout the ship.

Plate 39. Laundry Facilities

Texas had complete facilities to care for the clothing of its officers and men. The laundry, located on the port side of deck 2, outboard of No. 4 barbette, is currently undergoing restoration. Its primary task was to clean the officers' uniforms. The laundry also did the enlisted men's clothing on a cyclical schedule. This often combined large divisions, like the boiler rooms, with smaller ones, like the repair division. Many enlisted men did their own wash in buckets in the passageways. They then hung the clothing to dry in warm areas, such as the boiler uptake spaces on deck 3 or the evaporator room on deck 2. The ship's original washers, tubs, soap tank, starch kettle, extractors, and ironer were manufactured by the American Laundry Manufacturing Co. of New York. The tailor shop is located on the port side of deck 2, just around the corner from the soda fountain. The tailors repaired clothing, added or removed rank badges, and converted standard issue uniforms to fit and look better on the men. *Texas* also had a cobbler's shop, located on the port side of deck 3, outboard of No. 1 barbette.

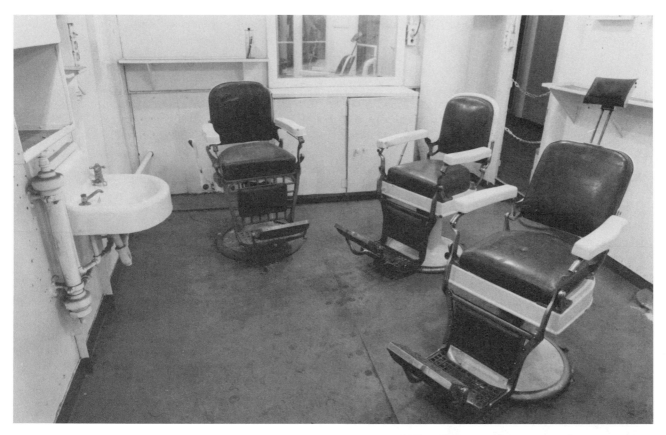

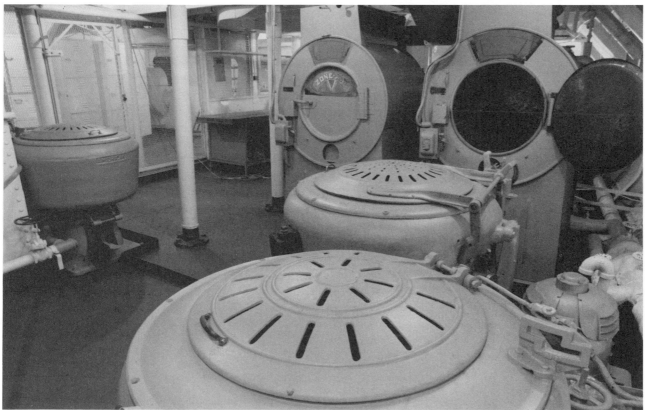

Plate 40. Brig

Even today, *Texas'* brig looks and feels like the most loathsome place on the ship. Located on the port side of deck 3, just outboard of No. 3 barbette, the brig had five cells, guarded by the ship's Marine contingent under the supervision of the master-at-arms. Prisoners ate the same food as the rest of the crew, unless the punishment specified bread and water. But there was no limit on the amount of bread and water, and such prisoners were checked regularly by a medical corpsman. Serious offenders awaiting court-martial were confined to the brig, but so were some men who committed minor infractions, providing brig time was specified in the table of punitive articles in the Uniform Code of Military Justice. At sea, the captain's word was law. Men could not refuse his non-judicial punishment while the ship was underway, though they could if stationed ashore or if the ship was in port. Minor infractions, such as being late for duty, brought a seaman before a Captain's Mast, accompanied by his division chief and department chief. The captain heard everyone's evidence and comments, then determined any necessary punishment from the punitive tables.

Plate 41. Engine Room Control Station

This view of the control station on the second level of *Texas'* starboard engine room amply demonstrates the complexity of the ship's propulsion plant. When funds were appropriated for construction of *Texas* and *New York,* most of the world's dreadnoughts were powered by steam turbine engines. In fact, the use of turbines in HMS *Dreadnought* was regarded as one of the most revolutionary aspects of that ship's design. But the United States Navy had reservations about the turbine by 1910, for two excellent reasons. First, U.S. warships spent long stretches at cruising speed and, especially in the Pacific, operated in waters far from their home bases. For that reason, economy and cruising range at speeds of ten to twelve knots, rather than maximum speed, were vital criteria to the navy. And second, turbines had been tried in previous classes of American dreadnoughts, most recently in the *Delaware* class, where the reciprocating-powered *Delaware* had outperformed *North Dakota,* a turbine-driven ship of the same class. So *Texas* and *New York* were built with two sets of four-cylinder, triple-expansion, reciprocating steam engines, constructed by the ship's builder, Newport News (Va.) Shipbuilding and Drydock Co.

Plate 42. Starboard Engine Detail

This detail shot isolates the starboard engine room's telegraph, which transmitted orders for changes in speed from either the bridge or armored conning tower. New incoming orders were announced over the noise of the heavy machinery by the gong shown just below the telegraph face. Behind the telegraph is the wall of one of the four giant cylinders that powered the vertical drive shafts. These in turn rotated the 142-foot-long propeller shaft. The legend on the cylinder wall shows that each engine developed 14,050 horsepower, a figure that enabled both *Texas* and *New York* to make easily their designed speed of twenty-one knots. In fact, the design of the ship and engines had allowed for a requirement of 32,000 combined horsepower, so in that sense, the navy's choice of reciprocating engines was a bargain. In addition, *Texas'* engine rooms were unusually spacious, sixty feet long and twenty-six feet, nine inches wide. This benefit reflected the navy's awareness that the reciprocating engine offered little further potential for development and that it might be replaced with turbines before the ship completed its service life. But neither *Texas* nor *New York* ever changed power plants.

Plate 43. Watertight Door

There was only one "shortest distance between two points" in *Texas'* engine rooms, and that was through this watertight door in the longitudinal bulkhead that divided the engine rooms through their first two levels. Bulkheads and watertight doors were as important to the survival of a dreadnought as its armor or guns. Together they subdivided the interior of the ship into many small compartments. Any one of these could be sealed off from the rest of the ship to prevent the spread of flooding from shell or torpedo hits. *Texas* had more than four hundred such compartments and the countless bulkheads needed to form them, but no bulkhead in the ship was more controversial than the one that divided the engine rooms. Rapid flooding in either large engine compartment from an underwater hit could cause a sizable list (slant) to one side or the other. The navy accepted this risk to obtain an advantage it considered more important—the continued operation of at least one engine in battle. It was also assumed that prompt counter-flooding of the void tanks on the side opposite the flooded compartment could rapidly correct the list. In addition, the navy could point to the use of such longitudinal bulkheads in virtually all European battleships of this period.

Plate 44. Chief Engineer's Station

Located on the second level of *Texas'* port engine room, facing the longitudinal bulkhead that divides the engine compartment, is the chief engineer's station. The chief engineer was totally responsible for the performance of the ship's power plant. Chief engineers were often older than many of their fellow officers, and their expertise with the engines bordered on the mystical. In *Texas* all that expertise was needed, for the ship's engines were a constant cause of complaint in the years between the world wars. Particularly noticeable were their severe torsional vibrations. These occurred, ironically, at the very cruising speeds for which they had been selected — the standard fleet speed of twelve to fourteen knots. Still, the engines did produce the statistical performance the navy wanted. *Texas* had a cruising radius of 7,060 miles at twelve knots with its reciprocating engines, while the Curtis turbines installed in earlier American dreadnoughts could do no better than 5,606 miles at the same speed. This range was insufficient to take American dreadnoughts from the west coast to the Philippines.

Plate 45. Boiler Rooms

The labyrinthine system of pipes and tubes that delivered power to *Texas'* engines is evident in this view of No. 4 boiler room. The boiler itself is the large, dark, triangular structure on the right side of the picture. Unlike the engine rooms, *Texas'* boiler rooms traversed the width of the ship and sit just three feet above the double-hulled bottom. Like most of its contemporaries, *Texas* began its service life as a coal-fired vessel, with fourteen Babcock & Wilcox boilers located in four firerooms. But fuel oil was far more efficient and much easier to resupply, and *Texas* was converted to oil-fired boilers during the 1925–27 refit. The ship received six new Bureau Express, three-drum boilers, two in each of three firerooms. The forward boiler room was freed for other purposes, and the coal storage bunkers along the sides of the ship were converted to crew's quarters. The new boiler rooms were quite spacious, a desirable situation for damage control. The oil-fired boilers provided 285 pounds per square inch of pressure at a temperature of 417 degrees. Horsepower remained the same. A full load of fuel oil weighed 5,200 tons, compared to 2,960 tons of coal with 400 tons of supplemental fuel oil prior to 1925.

Plate 46. Main Distribution Board Room

Located deep within *Texas* and well behind the thickest portion of the armored belt is the nerve center of the ship, the source of its electrical power, the main distribution board room. From here, electrical power is distributed throughout the ship for every function from food preparation to operating the guns that hurl three-quarter-ton shells at targets. The power itself is created by four 400-kilowatt, 120-volt direct-current generator sets, located in two dynamo rooms. One of these is located just below the main distribution board room, and the second is just aft of the boiler rooms, immediately below the secondary distribution board room. There is an interesting historical anomaly about *Texas'* electric supply. When the ship was built, the only electric power on warships was direct current (DC). But between the wars, safer, more efficient alternating current (AC)—the kind common in every American household—replaced DC. Dreadnoughts made the switch by installing DC-to-AC converters. These were turbines run by direct current, which in turn powered the generators that produced alternating current. Such converters have become rarities, and *Texas* has two of them.

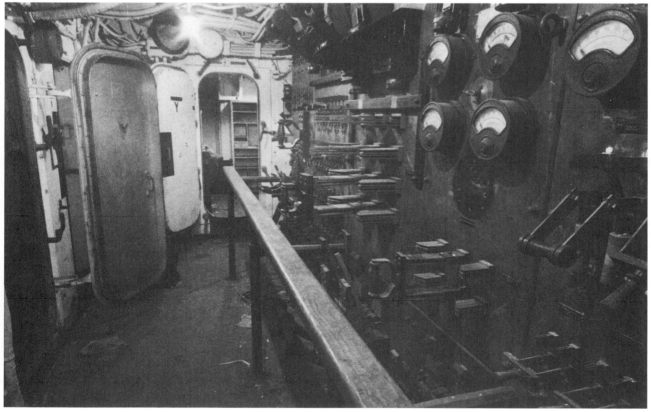

Plate 47. Evaporator Room

Whether coal- or oil-fired, *Texas'* boilers produced the same product to drive the ship's propellers: steam. The boilers functioned much like giant kettles, but they produced steam twenty-four hours a day and therefore were in constant need of water. That water came into *Texas* from the sea around it. Before it reached the boilers it was purified in the evaporator room on deck 2, just aft of the cafeteria area. The ship's boiler system required that its feed water be as pure as possible. Unpurified salt water would cake up the intricate boiler tubing. Worse, it might produce a hot spot, an area of uneven heating that could rupture a critical boiler line and reduce the ship's speed or bring it to a complete halt. After purification, the water was passed into the ship's feed water tanks, located in several different areas of the vessel. If water in a tank were in some way contaminated, that tank could be closed down, and feed water could be piped into the boilers from another tank without interruption in the ship's propulsion.

Plate 48. Steering Engine

Steering large ships looks so easy in the movies that most people never realize that it would be impossible for one person to manually move a rudder that is not only three stories tall but also located at the opposite end of the ship. The answer lies in a complex system of hydraulics that is obvious in only a few areas of *Texas*. The most visible display is located at the aft end of the starboard engine room, where a separate compartment houses the steering engine that controls the emergency movements of the rudder. Shown here is the complexity of the machinery needed to produce the near-instant maneuvers required by a large warship. *Texas* mounted just one balanced rudder, located on the centerline directly underneath the ship's stern. The helmsman, steering from either the navigation bridge or the armored conning tower, communicated the ship's course changes through both electrical and hydraulic lines. These lines were located in a protected wiring passage running through the center of the ship.

Plate 49. Propeller

Though its fuels changed, *Texas'* power plant drove the same two propellers throughout the ship's career. They had three blades, were 18 feet, 7¾ inches in diameter, and had a pitch of 19 feet, 11½ inches. (The "pitch" of a ship's propeller is the ideal distance forward any blade travels from its starting point to the completion of one full revolution.) The propeller shafts were turned directly by the reciprocating engines, and the outboard portion of each shaft was supported by two struts attached to the outer hull. The propellers turned in opposite directions from one another, to correct the torque that would have swung the ship's stern to one side or the other. Both *Texas* and *New York* used the same propeller design. *Texas'* props were removed from the ship in 1948, and one of them is on display adjacent to Route 134, Battleground Road, just above the ship's anchorage. Each propeller weighed approximately twenty-seven thousand pounds. The speed of warships is described in knots as well as revolutions, or turns of the propeller. Verbal commands for changes in speed are often given in revolutions, such as "Make 120 revolutions," which is approximately twenty knots.

Plate 50. *Texas* in Drydock

An inspection team, tiny figures against the right side of *Texas'* hull, give their work a final once-over as the ship sits in the "Big T" Drydock at Todd Shipyards' Galveston Division. *Texas* entered the drydock on December 13, 1988, and emerged in late February of 1990. The hull and outer structures were extensively restored, and the ship was given a new paint job that replicates the navy Camouflage Measure 21 it had at the end of World War II. The work, conducted under the direction of the Texas Parks and Wildlife Department, will ensure the ship's structural integrity well into the twenty-first century. The rounded bulges at the lower edges of the ship's hull are the anti-torpedo bulges added during the 1925–27 refit. The sixty-five-inch wide bulges, filled with oil or water, were designed to increase resistance to torpedo attack by absorbing the shock of the underwater explosion and putting more distance between the blast and the ship's vital machinery. The power of explosions is magnified underwater, so the torpedo had become the dreadnought's nemesis, and all major navies "bulged" their battleships during the interwar years. Because they altered the hull shape and increased the weight, the bulges reduced *Texas'* speed from 21 to 20.4 knots.

Glossary

abaft: Farther aft than astern of, as in "abaft the after tripod mast."

aft: Toward the rear of the ship.

air castle: Nickname for the open 5-inch gun casemates on both sides of *Texas'* upper deck.

amidships: In the middle of the ship.

anchor shank: The straight stem of the anchor to which the anchor chains are connected.

armored belt: A sheet of vertical steel plate many inches thick, the outer facing further hardened by carbonizing, located within the ship's hull to protect the vital machinery spaces from shellfire damage. *Texas'* belt is 12 inches thick.

athwartships: Across the ship, from side to side.

baffle: In dreadnoughts, systems within the ammunition magazines and hoists that prevent fire or flashes from igniting the magazine and blowing the ship apart.

barbette: A cylindrical, heavily armored tower that supports each main battery turret and protects the ammunition hoist system. On *Texas*, the barbettes extend to deck 3 and are 10–12 inches thick.

battlecruiser: Faster and often much larger than their battleship counterparts, the battlecruisers were of similar design and armament but were much more lightly armored. They were intended to be the fast scouting wing of the dreadnought fleets and to hunt enemy surface raiders. Unfortunately, they proved very vulnerable to shell fire.

battle line: The formation from which ships fought since the days of sail. Fleets lined up bow to stern opposite one another and pounded away with heavy cannon. Dreadnoughts were designed to do the same, but they seldom used the line-of-battle formation in its classic form.

battleship: Though used interchangably with "dreadnought" in this text, the "line-of-battleship" had been an integral part of navies since the days of sail. The term denoted a vessel large enough and carrying enough guns to take its place in the line of battle. A ship like HMS *Victory*, Adm. Horatio Nelson's seventy-four-gun flagship at Trafalgar, was a battleship, while a frigate with fewer than forty guns was not.

boilers: Operating in principle like giant teakettles, a dreadnought's boilers produced the steam needed to drive the engines, whether they were turbines or reciprocating engines like those on *Texas*.

boiler uptakes: Large tubes leading from each boiler to the ship's funnel. The uptakes carried the gaseous by-products of the boilers out of the ship's interior.

bow: The very front of a ship; its forward-most point.

breech: The rear chamber of the guns, into which the shells and propellant charges were loaded. The breech block, weighing several tons, then sealed the breech. This forced the gases of the ignited propellant to hurl the shell out the gun's muzzle.

bridge: The central command-and-control station on board a warship. The captain spends most of his time at sea here, the ship is steered from here, and orders for maneuvers or actions to be taken are issued from here. *Texas* has two bridges: the navigation bridge described above, and a flag bridge, from which admirals could direct entire fleets of ships.

brig: The ship's jail.

broadside: The firing of all the ship's main guns in unison at a single target. Weight of broadside was often relied upon as a measure of a ship's capabilities, though this proved a fallacy in battle. The weight of *Texas'* broadside was 15,000 pounds.

bulkhead: Interior walls of a ship, subdividing its interior into smaller compartments.

caliber: In large naval guns, the diameter of the bore, and an indicator of gun length. For example, *Texas'* 14-inch/45-caliber guns were 630 inches (14 × 45) or 52.5 feet long. Its 5-inch/51-caliber guns were 255 inches (5 × 51) or 21 feet, 3 inches long. More generally, caliber is an expression of the bore diameter in inches, for example, a .50-caliber machine gun has a bore diameter of one-half inch.

captain's mast: A limited court of inquiry, used when the ship is at sea. Crewmen accused of infractions of navy regulations are brought before the captain's mast. The captain alone determines guilt or innocence and punishment.

carbonizing: An expensive process for hardening the outer face of a dreadnought's armor by exposing it to carbon during manufacture. Carbonized armor was more likely to "defeat" an enemy shell by either deflecting it or exploding it before it penetrated the ship's interior.

casemate: Armored compartment for a gun and its crew. On *Texas*, 5-inch casemates were first located on the second deck. Later they became the "air castles" found today on the upper deck.

CIC: Acronym for Combat Information Center, located during World War II in a structure at the base of *Texas'* forward tripod mast. The center processed information on both surface and air targets and directed the fire of the ship's weapons.

citadel: That portion of the ship's interior enclosed by the armored belt and armored transverse bulkheads. It always included the ammunition handling areas and the engine and boiler rooms.

concentration dials: Part of *Texas'* early fire-control equipment, these large, clock-like dials were located on both masts. They showed the range at which *Texas* was firing so that other ships, whose view was obscured, could concentrate their fire on the same target.

conning tower: A heavily armored command station, located near the navigation bridge and used by senior officers in battle.

cordite: The most common propellant charge used in dreadnought guns during both world wars. It was stored in silk bags, which burned more evenly than other materials.

division: All those men working in one area, such as gun crews, or performing one specialized function, such as repair.

dreadnought: Umbrella term for a type of battleship that presented revolutionary increases in size, speed, gun power, and protection. The first such ship, HMS *Dreadnought*, was launched by the British Royal Navy in 1906. It revolutionized naval construction and set off the first great arms race centered on one weapon. The 1906 *Dreadnought* was the ninth ship in the history of the Royal Navy to carry that name.

executive officer: The second-in-command on a warship. Often referred to as "the Ex-oh" (American), or "Number one" (British).

fantail: Used in conjunction with port or starboard, it designates a location on the stern, or rear, part of the ship's upper deck, along one side or the other.

fathom: A nautical measure of depth, representing six feet.

foremast: The mast closest to the front of the ship.

forward: Toward the front of the ship.

14-inch guns: The main armament of *Texas*, the measurement indicates the diameter of the gun's bore.

funnel: The ship's smokestack.

geedunk: Navy slang for sweets, such as ice cream or pastries.

gunhouse: The section of the turret system containing the guns. It sits atop the barbette and rotates to train the guns on a target.

gun sleeve: A section of the gunhouse containing one gun.

halyards: Rope lines from which signal flags send visual messages to other ships.

hawse pipe: Housing piercing the forward part of the upper deck through the side of the hull into which the shank of the anchor is drawn when the ship is underway.

Jutland: (pronounced Yoot-land) German name for Denmark, also given to the first and only battle involving massed fleets of dreadnoughts. Fought in the late afternoon of May 31, 1916, and the early hours of June 1, the battle produced no clear-cut winner. Germany claimed a tactical victory, because the British lost more ships and men. But strategically, Britain was the ultimate victor. The Grand Fleet's blockade of German ports remained in effect, and the German fleet never sortied at full strength again during World War I.

kamikaze: Japanese for "divine wind," it was the name taken by Japan's suicide pilots who attempted to ram their planes into American warships in the late stages of World War II.

keel: A ship's spine, a huge beam that runs the length of the hull, on which the rest of the vessel's structure is built. Laying the keel is the first step in any ship construction.

knot: A nautical measure of speed, equivalent to 1.1516 miles per hour on land.

liberty: Naval term for shore leave.

list: Slant or lean of a ship from its vertical axis, usually after battle damage floods compartments on one side of the vessel.

magazines: Ammunition storage area on a ship. Each of *Texas'* five 14-inch gun turrets has its own magazine.

mainmast: Mast nearest the center of the ship. In the days of sail, also the tallest mast. But *Texas'* mainmast is the shorter of its tripods.

mess: Areas on a ship where the men take their meals.

muzzle velocity: The speed at which a shell exists the gun barrel, expressed in feet per second.

outboard of: Phrase identifying the location of compartments immediately adjacent to the outer hull wall and across a passageway from some other landmark. (e.g. "The ship's surgery is located outboard of No. 4 barbette.")

padeye: A ring that can be inserted and later removed from any heavy object.

port: The left side of a ship when facing the bow, it remains the port side when facing the stern.

propellor pitch: Under ideal circumstances, the distance forward any one propellor blade moves in a single complete turn.

quad mount: Mount with four guns.

revolutions: Turns of the propellor; also a description of speed. On *Texas*, 120 revolutions equaled 20 knots.

sortie: Both a verb and a noun, it refers to a ship's leaving port on a mission.

starboard: Opposite of port; the right side of the ship when facing the bow.

stanchion: Support columns in the interior of the ship.

stern: Rear-most point on a ship.

superstructure: Built-up forward area on the ship's upper deck, containing the bridges, fire control areas, and other command-and-control stations.

train: Turning of a gun mount to point at a target.

transverse: Bulkheads built at right angles to the keel.

void tanks: Hull compartments purposely kept empty so that they can be flooded to adjust the ship's trim or correct a list from battle damage.

Vichy: Provisional capital of France under German occupation after June, 1940. It included the French North African colonies.

Washington Naval Treaty of 1922: First of three treaties to limit the number, size, and gun power of dreadnoughts. The treaty also established the "life" of dreadnoughts at twenty years and declared a ten-year moratorium on their construction.

working chamber: Compartment located immediately under the gunhouse, where training, elevation, and depression of the guns was controlled.

zeppelin: German-built rigid-frame airship, or dirigible. Used by the German High Seas fleet as scouts, they represented the first real threat to the dreadnought by aviation.

Appendix A: Battleship *Texas* (BB35) in Profile

Builder: Newport News (Va.) Shipbuilding and Drydock Co.
Authorized: 1910
Keel Laid: April 17, 1911
Launched: May 18, 1912
Commissioned: March 12, 1914

Displacement:	**as built**	**in 1945**
Normal tons	27,000	29,500
Full load tons	28,400	32,000
Dimensions:		
Length at waterline	565 ft.	565 ft.
Length overall	573 ft.	573 ft.
Beam	95.25 ft.	106.25 ft.
Draught	28.5 ft.	31.5 ft.
Armament:		
14-inch/45 caliber	10 (5×2)	10 (5×2)
5-inch/51 caliber	21	6
3-inch antiaircraft	n/a	10
40mm antiaircraft	n/a	40
20mm antiaircraft	n/a	44
Torpedo tubes (21-inch)	4	n/a
Aircraft	n/a	3
Armor:		
Side—main belt	10–12 inches	n/c
Side—ends	6 inches	n/c
Decks—main	1.5–2.5 inches	n/c
Decks—lower	2.5–3.5 inches	n/c
14-inch turrets—faces	14 inches	n/c
14-inch turrets—tops	4 inches	n/c
14-inch turrets—sides	8–9 inches	n/c
14-inch turrets—rear	8 inches	n/c
14-inch turret barbettes	5–12 inches	n/c
Casemates	6.5–11 inches	n/c
Conning tower—walls	12 inches	n/c
Conning tower—top	4 inches	n/c
Conning tower—tube	11 inches	n/c

Machinery:	as built	in 1945
Boilers—type	Babcock & Wilcox	Bureau Express
Boilers—number	14	6
Engines	2 vertical inverted direct-acting, 4-cylinder triple expansion, known familiarly as reciprocating engines, manufactured by the shipbuilder.	
Shafts	2	2
Propellers	2 3-bladed, 18⅔' in diameter	
Performance:		
Shaft horsepower—design	28,100	28,100
Shaft horsepower—trial	28,373	n/a
Maximum speed—design	21.0 knots	20.4 knots
Maximum speed—trial	21.05 knots	n/a
Range—nautical miles	8,400 at 10 knots	
Fuel Capacity:		
Coal	2,960 tons max.	n/a
Oil	400 tons	5,200 tons
Crew Complement:		
Officers	58	98
Enlisted men	944	1,625
Marines—officers	n/a	2
Marines—enlisted	n/a	82

Appendix B:
Ship's Commanding Officers

Albert Grant, Captain, USN (March 12, 1914–June 10, 1915)

John Hood, Captain, USN (June 10, 1915–August 14, 1916)

Victor Blue, Captain, USN (August 14, 1916–December 31, 1918)

Nathan C. Twining, Captain, USN (December 31, 1918–July 17, 1919)

Frank H. Schofield, Captain, USN (July 17, 1919–June 17, 1921)

Edward S. Kellog, Captain, USN (June 17, 1921–July 6, 1922)

Andre M. Proctor, Captain, USN (July 6, 1922–May 22, 1924)

Ivan C. Wettengel, Captain, USN (May 22, 1924–September 28, 1925)

Charles A. Blakely, Captain, USN (September 28, 1925–June 2, 1926)

Zeno E. Biggs, Captain, USN (June 2, 1926–January 4, 1928)

Joseph R. Defrees, Captain, USN (January 4, 1928–July 9, 1929)

Adolphus Andrews, Captain, USN (July 9, 1929–May 13, 1931)

Julius C. Townsend, Captain, USN (May 13, 1931–June 17, 1933)

Lamar R. Leahy, Captain, USN (June 17, 1933–April 15, 1935)

Sherwood A. Taffinder, Captain, USN (April 15, 1935–November 21, 1936)

Fred Fremont Rogers, Captain, USN (November 21, 1936–June 1, 1938)

Robert R. M. Emmet, Captain, USN (June 1, 1938–May 31, 1940)

Clarence N. Hinkamp, Captain, USN (May 31, 1940–August 2, 1941)

Lewis W. Comstock, Captain, USN (August 2, 1941–September 28, 1942)

William E. Hennigar, Commander, USN (September 28, 1942–October 3, 1942)

Lawrence Wild, Captain, USN (October 3, 1942–October 14, 1942)

William E. Hennigar, Commander, USN (October 14, 1942–October 17, 1942)

Roy Pfaff, Captain, USN (October 17, 1942–March 10, 1944)

Charles A. Baker, Captain, USN (March 10, 1944–August 17, 1945)

Gerald L. Schetky, Captain, USN (August 17, 1945–July 3, 1946)

Robert N. Downes, Commander, USN (July 3, 1946–March 6, 1947)

James R. Bagshaw, Jr., Captain, USNR (March 6, 1947–April 7, 1947)

Samuel J. McKee, Commander, USN (April 7, 1947–July 31, 1947)

Jack Seward, Lieutenant Commander, USN (July 31, 1947–April 21, 1948)

Charles A. Baker, Captain, USN (April 21, 1948, the day the ship was presented to the state)

Suggested Further Reading

GENERAL

Hough, Richard. *Dreadnought: A History of the Modern Battleship.* New York: Bonanza Books, 1975. The best available overview of the dreadnought era, for those more interested in the history than the technology.

————. *The Great War at Sea, 1914–1918.* Oxford: Oxford University Press, 1986. A fascinating study of the war the dreadnoughts were built to fight, and the men who would not let them fight it.

————. *The Longest Battle: The War at Sea, 1939–45.* New York: William Morrow and Company, 1986. A necessary and well-written companion to the World War I volume.

Mclean, Anne, and Suzanne Poole, eds. *Fighting Ships of World Wars One and Two.* New York: Crescent Books, 1976. Particularly interesting for its detailed maps and account of the Battle of Jutland.

Mason, Theodore C. *Battleship Sailor.* Annapolis, Md.: Naval Institute Press, 1982. A fascinating look at both life aboard a dreadnought and life in the U.S. Navy before World War II.

Middlebrook, Martin, and Patrick Mahoney. *Battleship: The Sinking of the Prince of Wales and the Repulse.* New York: Charles Scribner's Sons, 1977. Detailed description of the moment the world knew the dreadnought era had ended.

von Mullenheim-Rechberg, Baron Burkhard. *Battleship Bismarck: A Survivor's Story.* Annapolis, Md.: Naval Institute Press, 1980. Not only the best real sea-chase yarn on record, but an interesting view of battleship life from the losing side.

TECHNICAL

Burt, R. A. *British Battleships of World War One.* Annapolis, Md.: Naval Institute Press, 1986. From *Dreadnought* and the battlecruisers to the hybrids that eventually became aircraft carriers.

Friedman, Norman. *U.S. Battleships: A Design History.* Annapolis, Md.: Naval Institute Press, 1987. A comprehensive and very readable look at U.S. dreadnought designs.

Hodges, Peter. *The Big Gun: Battleship Armament, 1860–1945.* Annapolis, Md.: Naval Institute Press, 1981. A complete, though heavily technical, look at the very reason for the dreadnoughts —their guns.

Lyon, Hugh. *The Encyclopedia of the World's Warships.* New York:

Crescent Books, 1978. The statistics are complete and the drawings particularly useful in understanding dreadnought layout.

Sturton, Ian. *Conway's All the World's Battleships: 1906 to the Present.* Annapolis, Md.: Naval Institute Press, 1987. Vital overview of every dreadnought built for every navy in the world.

Index

Battleship Texas was composed into type on a Compugraphic digital phototypesetter in eleven point Trump Medieval with two points of spacing between the lines. Trump Medieval was also selected for display. The book was designed by Jim Billingsley, typeset by Metricomp, Inc., and printed offset by Hart Graphics, Inc. The paperback books were bound by Hart Graphics, Inc. The cloth bound books were bound by John H. Dekker & Sons, Inc. The paper on which this book is printed carries acid-free characteristics for an effective life of at least three hundred years.

TEXAS A&M UNIVERSITY PRESS : COLLEGE STATION